To:

_____

From:

THe
P✿wer
OF A
P☺sitive
M♥M

Devotional & Journal

About the Author

Best-selling author Karol Ladd offers lasting hope and biblical truth to women around the world through her positive book series. A gifted communicator and dynamic leader, Karol is founder and president of Positive Life Principles, Inc., a resource company offering strategies for success in both home and work. Her vivacious personality makes her a popular speaker to women's organizations, church groups and corporate events. She is co-founder of a character-building club for young girls called USA Sonshine Girls and serves on several educational boards. Karol is a frequent guest on radio and television programs. Her most valued role is that of wife to Curt and mother to daughters Grace and Joy. Visit her Web site at PositiveLifePrinciples.com.

52
Monday
Morning
Motivations

THe
P❀wer
OF A
P☺sitive
M♥M

Devotional & Journal

Karol Ladd

HOWARD BOOKS
A DIVISION OF SIMON & SCHUSTER

NEW YORK LONDON TORONTO SIDNEY

OUR PURPOSE AT HOWARD BOOKS IS TO:

- *Increase* faith in the hearts of growing Christians
- *Inspire* holiness in the lives of believers
- *Instill* hope in the hearts of struggling people everywhere

BECAUSE HE'S COMING AGAIN!

Published by Howard Books, a division of Simon & Schuster
1230 Avenue of the Americas, New York, NY 10020

HOWARD
BOOKS

The Power of a Positive Mom Devotional and Journal © 2006 by Karol Ladd

All rights reserved, including the right to reproduce this book or portions thereof in any form whatsoever. For information address Howard Books, 3117 North 7th Street, West Monroe, Louisiana 71291-2227.

10   9   8   7   6   5   4   3

Interior design by Richard Foshee
Cover design by Stephanie Walker

Library of Congress Cataloging-in-Publication Data
Ladd, Karol.
    The power of a positive mom devotional; : 52 Monday morning motivations /
    Karol Ladd,
        p.cm.
    ISBN 1-58229-486-0; ISBN 1-4165-3396-6
    1. Mothers—Prayer-books and devotions—English. 2. Devotional calendars.
    I. Title.

    BV4847.L34 2006
    242'.6431—dc22

                                                                        2005054927

HOWARD is a registered trademark of Simon & Schuster, Inc.

Manufactured in the United States of America

For information regarding special discounts for bulk purchases, please contact Simon & Schuster Special Sales at 1-800-456-6798 or business@simonandschuster.com.

Scripture quotations are taken from the *Holy Bible, New Living Translation,* copyright © 1996. Used by permission of Tyndale House Publishers, Inc., Wheaton, Illinois 60189. All rights reserved.

Contents

Introduction 1

Week 1   Created in His Image 4

Week 2   "I Will Help You" 8

Week 3   The Grace Challenge 12

Week 4   From Grumbling to Gratitude 16

Week 5   The Beauty of God's Love 20

Week 6   Courage and Commitment 24

Week 7   Who Gets the Glory? 28

Week 8   Rich and Rewarding Loyalty 32

Week 9   Delighting in God's Blessings 36

Week 10   God Is Our Provider 40

Week 11   The Battle Is the Lord's 44

Week 12   God's Glorious Restoration 48

Week 13   Big Task, Big Testimony 52

Week 14   Out of the Comfort Zone 56

Week 15   Trusting God 60

Week 16   Delighting in the Lord 64

Week 17   The Power of Our Words 68

Week 18   A Time and a Season 72

Week 19   Beautiful Passion 76

Week 20   His Glorious Strength 80

Week 21   God's Perfect Plan 84

Week 22   Great Is His Faithfulness! 88

Week 23   A Beautiful, New Heart 92

Week 24   A Life That Points to God 96

Contents

Week 25	Love beyond Limits	100
Week 26	A Heart of Repentance	104
Week 27	God's Plumb Line	108
Week 28	We Can't Hide from God	112
Week 29	The Depths of God's Forgiveness	116
Week 30	Strength for the Journey	120
Week 31	His Own Special Treasure	124
Week 32	Why Worry?	128
Week 33	The Beauty of Service	132
Week 34	One Baby, One Night	136
Week 35	The Ultimate Travel Information	140
Week 36	We Are Not Alone	144
Week 37	Nothing Can Separate Us	148
Week 38	Troubles to Triumph	152
Week 39	Love That Builds Up	156
Week 40	Victory over Anger	160
Week 41	Experiencing Joy and Peace	164
Week 42	A View of Eternity	168
Week 43	Positive Principles for Life	172
Week 44	Family Resemblance	176
Week 45	Woman to Woman	180
Week 46	The Joy of Generosity	184
Week 47	A Gracious Invitation	188
Week 48	Opportunities to Trust God	192
Week 49	His Divine Power at Work	196
Week 50	The Power of Love	200
Week 51	Reaching Out with Mercy	204
Week 52	A Longing for Heaven	208

Introduction

It's Monday morning. You'd love to stay in bed and enjoy just a few more minutes of treasured rest or blissful peace and quiet—but that's not an option at this stage in your life. Maybe you have toddlers tugging at you, or a baby crying for you, or teenagers calling your name. Whatever the case, the morning rush is about to begin, and there's no getting around it.

Let's be honest. For moms the Monday morning routine is not always a welcomed one. That's why I wrote this devotional. I want it to be your Monday morning blessing! My desire is to walk through God's Word with you, mom to mom, once a week for the next fifty-two weeks. Why? Because the Bible is rich with wisdom and overflowing with practical, powerful tools for living a full, contented, positive life as a mom, whether your kids are in diapers or in high school. By starting off each Monday with a motivational message designed for moms that comes straight from the Word of God, my hope is that you'll find the encouragement, help, and spiritual fuel you'll need for the week ahead.

The fact that you're reading these words lets me know that you, like me, want to be a positive mom who creates a positive environment of love, encouragement, and care in your home. But we can't do it on our own. We have our strengths, to be sure; but we also have our weaknesses. We all make mistakes. And we all need God's help! In fact, the

Introduction

first step to becoming a truly positive mom is recognizing that we don't have everything it takes to be positive in and of ourselves. We need God's power at work in our lives.

This devotional offers a unique journey through the Bible that will help us tap into that power. We begin in Genesis and move on to passages from almost every book of the Bible, all the way to Revelation. Since there are sixty-six books and we only have fifty-two weeks, we won't quite cover them all. But we will get a taste of most of them as we walk our way through God's Word.

I have to tell you, my love for the Lord was renewed and strengthened through the process of studying and preparing the devotionals in this book. From Genesis to Revelation, my heart was touched by the common thread of God's redeeming love and mercy toward his people. My prayer is that you, too, will be strengthened and renewed as you walk with me through the pages of this book; that you grow to love God more each day; and that you'll allow him to gently guide you according to the wisdom and life principles he provides in his Word.

You will notice that in each day's devotional, I've provided room for you to record your thoughts and prayer requests for the week. I've included a sample prayer you may want to use as a guide in your own prayer time, along with a suggestion for further reading that will allow you to delve deeper into God's Word on a particular topic. I've also added some powerful quotes by great leaders and godly heroes who've gone before us—statements that have motivated me as a mom, and I trust will motivate you too.

Introduction

In addition, I have included a series of suggested choices you may want to consider during the week—choices related to the day's topic that have the potential to impact your home in a positive way. I also leave space for you to write your own thoughts on specific, personal choices you want to make, based on what you've seen that day in God's Word. After all, life is all about choices. To be positive moms, we need to make wise choices for ourselves and our families each day. Most of those day-to-day choices may seem small and insignificant at the time; but added together, they have the potential to make a big difference not only in our lives, but in the lives of our children and family members.

So let's agree to meet together at least once a week through the pages of this book. Although the subtitle is *Fifty-Two Monday Morning Motivations*, you don't have to reserve these devotionals for Mondays only. My intention is to give you a weekly boost of encouragement to help you become a positive and successful mom all week long. But you can read these devotionals any day of the week, and even throughout the week. Use them in whatever way works best for your life.

Meanwhile, I encourage you to meet with your heavenly Father every day in further Bible study and prayer. Remember, you are not alone! The Lord is always with you, ready to help you, strengthen you, and guide you. Enjoy his presence as you read, study, and consider his Word to you. He will give you power to become a positive mom who makes a positive impact in the lives of those you love.

Created in His Image

 Key Scripture: Genesis 1:27–31

So God created people in his own image; God patterned them after himself; male and female he created them. God blessed them and told them, "Multiply and fill the earth and subdue it. Be masters over the fish and birds and all the animals." And God said, "Look! I have given you the seed-bearing plants throughout the earth and all the fruit trees for your food. And I have given all the grasses and other green plants to the animals and birds for their food." And so it was. Then God looked over all he had made, and he saw that it was excellent in every way.

What we believe about God is the most important thing about us.

A. W. TOZER

Created in His Image

Mom's Reflection

Amazing! "God created people in his own image," and his creation was "excellent in every way"! The power of these truths can have a tremendous impact in our lives and in the lives of our children.

Think about it: we are created in the image of almighty God! Perhaps you don't feel so God-like all the time. Me neither. But "created in his image" (quite obviously) doesn't mean that we are exactly like God in all his supernatural power and splendor. Rather, it means we are a reflection of his person and character. We can reason. We can show love, patience, kindness, and forgiveness. We have a soul, which sets us apart from the rest of creation.

When we are tempted to think, *I just don't have what it takes to be a good mom* or *God must have made a mistake when he made me*, we can rest in the assurance that God has created us—and he did so in an excellent way. Our worth is based on the fact that we have been made by God himself to be like him! Knowing that we bear God's image ought to give us a positive view of ourselves and others, including our children and family members. Let us not criticize what God has made, but rather rejoice in his creation, knowing that he makes no mistakes.

Week 1

 ## My Thoughts

In what ways do I see myself as a unique and special creation of God? _____

_____

_____

_____

_____

_____

My Prayer

"Glorious Creator, marvelous Father, thank you for the way you created me and each and every one of my family members. Thank you for caring so much about mankind that you formed us in your image. I rejoice in your excellent creation! Help me to love and bless my kids, recognizing that they are a reflection of your image. May they begin to grasp the wonderful fact that they have been created in an excellent way for your glory. In Jesus's name I pray, amen."

This week I'm praying for: _____

_____

_____

_____

_____

_____

My Choices

- This week I will choose to rejoice in the fact that I am created in God's image.

- This week I will choose to encourage my children to know that they are made by God in an excellent way.

- This week I will choose to enjoy every person who crosses my path as a unique creation of God.

- This week I will choose to:_____

_____

_____

_____

_____

_____

For Further Reading: Genesis 1–3

> Though you are one of the
> teeming millions in this world,
> and though the world would have
> you believe that you do not count
> and that you are but a speck in
> the mass, God says, "I know you."
>
> D. MARTYN LLOYD-JONES

"I Will Help You"

 Key Scripture: Exodus 4:10–12

But Moses pleaded with the LORD, "O Lord, I'm just not a good speaker. I never have been, and I'm not now, even after you have spoken to me. I'm clumsy with words."

"Who makes mouths?" The LORD asked him. "Who makes people so they can speak or not speak, hear or not hear, see or not see? Is it not I, the LORD? Now go, and do as I have told you. I will help you speak well, and I will tell you what to say."

Without the assistance of the Divine Being . . . I cannot succeed. With that assistance, I cannot fail.

ABRAHAM LINCOLN

"I Will Help You"

 ## Mom's Reflection

It's so easy for us, like Moses, to focus on what we can't do—or perhaps don't want to do. Over time those negatives can grow into mountains of worry, concern, and confinement. We build our own prisons with the bars of "I can't": "I can't cope with the kids." "I can't teach them well." "I can't get it all done." The list can go on and on.

The question is, what is God calling you to do? He will help you. As a friend of mine always says, "Where God guides, he provides." Moses needed to heed those words and trust in God's strength, rather than focusing on what he couldn't do in his own strength. As moms we need to hear God's voice saying to us, "You may not be able to do it on your own, but I made you. I know what you need, and I can help you." Whenever you are tempted to think, *I just can't do it*, remember that as God leads you, he will give you what you need. He made you and he is able to equip you for the job.

My Thoughts

Do I trust God to be my strength in my weaknesses? What "I can'ts" do I need to give over to him? _____

_____

_____

_____

_____

_____

My Prayer

"O wonderful Lord, you have called me to be a mother. You have given me a monumental and magnificent job! But I can't do it alone; I don't have what it takes. I need you. I need your equipping. Help me to replace my 'I can't' with 'but God can.' Help me to follow you and only do what you are calling me to do in your strength. Thank you for creating me and caring for me. May my life glorify you! In Jesus's name I pray, amen."

This week I'm praying for:_____

_____

_____

_____

_____

_____

"I Will Help You"

 **My Choices**

- This week I will choose to focus on what God can do, not what I can't do.

- This week I will choose to seek God's leadership and guidance.

- This week I will choose to ask him for help in all the tasks I undertake.

- This week I will choose to: _____

_____

_____

_____

_____

_____

 For Further Reading: Exodus 3–4

> Walk boldly and wisely . . . There is a
> hand above that will help you on.
>
> PHILIP JAMES BAILEY

11

The Grace Challenge

 Key Scripture: Leviticus 19:16–18

"Do not spread slanderous gossip among your people.

"Do not try to get ahead at the cost of your neighbor's life, for I am the LORD.

"Do not nurse hatred in your heart for any of your relatives.

"Confront your neighbors directly so you will not be held guilty for their crimes.

"Never seek revenge or bear a grudge against anyone, but love your neighbor as yourself. I am the LORD."

Lord, give us grace and strength to forbear and to persevere. Give us courage and gaiety and the quiet mind, spare to us our friends, soften to us our enemies.

ROBERT LOUIS STEVENSON

Mom's Reflection

With thousands of Israelites trudging together through an unknown wilderness, a plan for civility was essential. The people had a long way to go, and they would never make it to the Promised Land if they turned on one another. So in the book of Leviticus, God provided laws for dealing with both people and circumstances. As you can see from the brief passage we just quoted, those laws of civility and decency were not always easy ones to follow. Yet if we as mothers were to employ even a few of these laws in our relationships today, we would be so much better for it!

As Christians, of course, we are no longer under the rule of Levitical law; we are under grace, thanks to Christ's sacrifice on the cross for us. As recipients of God's glorious grace, then, we ought to be showering grace on others in turn. And what does grace toward others look like? I think it looks a lot like today's passage. Guarding our mouths from gossip, forgiving, not holding grudges—all of these are practical ways we can shed God's grace on the people around us. Let's teach our kids, through our words and our example, to reflect on the goodness of God's wonderful grace and, in turn, to offer that grace to others.

My Thoughts

In what ways do I need to show God's grace toward others in my life? _____

_____

_____

_____

_____

My Prayer

"God of grace and mercy, thank you for pouring your grace on me through the sacrifice of your Son. I praise you that through faith in Jesus, I am forgiven. Help me now to forgive others. Guard my mouth from gossip and my heart from grudges. Teach me to be a conduit of your grace, so that grace flows freely through me to my family members and all the other people in my life. Thank you for your Word and the direction it gives for living and loving in grace. In Jesus's name I pray, amen."

This week I'm praying for: _____

_____

_____

_____

_____

The Grace Challenge

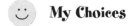 **My Choices**

- This week I will choose to focus on God's great love and grace toward me.

- This week I will choose to show grace toward others.

- This week I will choose to ask God's help in guarding my heart and mind.

- This week I will choose to: _____

_____

_____

_____

_____

 For Further Reading: Ephesians 4:28–32

Sanctification is the work
of God's free grace, whereby
we are renewed in the whole man
after the image of God, and are
enabled more and more to die unto
sin and live unto righteousness.

WESTMINSTER CATECHISM

From Grumbling to Gratitude

 Key Scripture: Numbers 14:26–30

Then the LORD said to Moses and Aaron, "How long will this wicked nation complain about me? I have heard everything the Israelites have been saying. Now tell them this: 'As surely as I live, I will do to you the very things I heard you say. I, the LORD, have spoken! You will all die here in this wilderness! Because you complained against me, none of you who are twenty years old or older and were counted in the census will enter the land I swore to give you. The only exceptions will be Caleb son of Jephunneh and Joshua son of Nun.'"

Gratitude to God makes even a temporal blessing a taste of heaven.

WILLIAM ROMAINE

From Grumbling to Gratitude

 Mom's Reflection

Complain, complain, complain! It became a habit for the Israelites in the wilderness. God gave them victory against their enemies and a miraculous delivery from slavery in Egypt. He provided food and water for them daily. The Bible even says their shoes didn't wear out! Yet they doubted God's goodness and chose to complain. As you can see from this passage, God wasn't too pleased with their almost unanimous lack of trust. Only two men, Joshua and Caleb, had faith in God's ability to provide for all their needs.

It's easy for us, as moms, to complain about people or circumstances. But have you ever viewed your complaining and whining as a lack of trust in God's provision? How would your life be different right now if you changed your grumbling to gratitude? Take a moment to thank God for what he has done and will do for you and your family. Granted, life in the wilderness wasn't Pleasure Island, but it wasn't slavery in Egypt either. Likewise, your life may not be the dream you always thought it would be; but God is with you, and he will provide for you. Decide today to keep your eyes on him instead of your circumstances.

My Thoughts

In what areas do I need to change my grumbling into gratitude? _____

_____

_____

_____

_____

_____

♡ My Prayer

"Dear Lord, you are my provider. Thank you for taking care of all my needs. Thank you for always being with me and never leaving me. I'm sorry for the times I have complained, when I should have been focusing on your goodness and mercy. Help me to replace my complaining with thanksgiving for all your blessings. Turn my eyes away from my problems and on to you. Help me to teach my children to do the same. In Jesus's name I pray, amen."

This week I'm praying for: _____

_____

_____

_____

_____

_____

From Grumbling to Gratitude

 My Choices

- This week I will choose to take my eyes off what is wrong in my life and look at what is right.
- This week I will choose to replace my grumbling with gratitude.
- This week I will choose to encourage my kids to see God's blessings all around us.
- This week I will choose to: _____

_____

_____

_____

_____

 For Further Reading: Numbers 14

Gratitude takes three forms:
a feeling in the heart,
an expression in words,
and a giving in return.

JOHN WANAMAKER

The Beauty of God's Love

 Key Scripture: Deuteronomy 7:7–9

The LORD did not choose you and lavish his love on you because you were larger or greater than other nations, for you were the smallest of all nations! It was simply because the LORD loves you, and because he was keeping the oath he had sworn to your ancestors. That is why the LORD rescued you with such amazing power from your slavery under Pharaoh in Egypt. Understand, therefore, that the LORD your God is indeed God. He is the faithful God who keeps his covenant for a thousand generations and constantly loves those who love him and obey his commands.

God does not love us because we are valuable, but we are valuable because God loves us.

MARTIN LUTHER

The Beauty of God's Love

 Mom's Reflection

What a beautiful love note to God's people—and to you and me! God lavishes his love on us, not because we have achieved any great status or because we are the most efficient, effective, and successful moms in the world. No, he loves us because we are his children, adopted into his family through faith in Christ. The Bible says he is faithful to keep his covenant of nonstop love toward us.

Aren't you blessed to know that the powerful God of all Creation, the God who made you, faithfully loves you each and every day? On those days when you feel less than lovable (maybe you yelled at the kids, or you snapped at a friend, or you complained to your husband about your work load), remember that God's love is faithful and abundant. It's not based on your performance but solely upon his grace. Feel his warm embrace and know that you are completely loved by him. There's nothing you can do to lose that love!

As moms let's take time to relish God's love for us. As we do we'll find it easier and easier to pour that same love out on the people around us.

Week 5

 My Thoughts

Do I live my daily life with the constant awareness that God deeply loves me? _____

_____

_____

_____

_____

My Prayer

"Loving and faithful heavenly Father, I praise you for your redeeming love and mercy toward me. I am amazed that you, the High King of Heaven, want to have a relationship with me! Thank you for being so faithful and loving. Thank you for allowing me to be a part of your family and keeping your covenant with me. I love you! Help me to share your love with my children and with all the other people in my life. In Jesus's name I pray, amen."

This week I'm praying for:_____

_____

_____

_____

_____

_____

The Beauty of God's Love

😊 My Choices

- This week I will choose to relish and reflect on God's great love toward me.

- This week I will choose to show God's love to others in my words and actions.

- This week I will choose to help my children understand the beauty of God's love.

- This week I will choose to: _____

_____

_____

_____

_____

 For Further Reading: Deuteronomy 6–7

Lord, send us such a flood-tide of Thy love that we shall be washed beyond the mire of doubt and fear.

CHARLES H. SPURGEON

Courage and Commitment

 Key Scripture: Joshua 1:7–9

Be strong and very courageous. Obey all the laws Moses gave you. Do not turn away from them, and you will be successful in everything you do. Study this Book of the Law continually. Meditate on it day and night so you may be sure to obey all that is written in it. Only then will you succeed. I command you—be strong and courageous! Do not be afraid or discouraged. For the LORD your God is with you wherever you go.

Courage is not simply one of the virtues, but the form of every virtue at the testing point.

C. S. LEWIS

Courage and Commitment

 ## Mom's Reflection

If you're like me, sometimes you don't feel "strong and courageous." Worries and fears creep in and take the place of strength and peace. In this week's passage we read that Joshua was about to face a fear-filled task: he was chosen by God to lead the Israelites into the Promised Land. Interestingly, God didn't suggest that Joshua be strong and courageous; he *commanded* it. Then he encouraged Joshua by saying, "I am with you wherever you go." What a powerful statement! We may not know what's on the road up ahead for ourselves and our families, but we do know that God will be with us every step of the way. We don't have to be afraid!

God also told Joshua to continually study and obey all the laws of Moses. Why? It takes courage to obey God and stand up for what's right. Studying and meditating on God's Word strengthens our spirits and gives us the courage we need to do what God has called us to do. You see, Scripture not only tells us how to live; it reminds us that God is with us. We can be strong and courageous, like Joshua, because our God is with us wherever we go.

My Thoughts

Am I regularly meditating on God's Word? How can I study
the Bible more diligently? _____

_____

_____

_____

_____

My Prayer

"Great and mighty Lord, I praise you for always being with
me. You guard me and protect me like a Good Shepherd.
Thank you for your presence! Keep me from being overcome
with fear; fill me with your peace instead. Help me to be
strong and courageous in my role as a mother. Thank you
for your Word and the power it has to transform my life.
Help me to study it, meditate on it, and obey it, so that I
can be successful in everything you have called me to do. In
Jesus's name I pray, amen."

This week I'm praying for:_____

_____

_____

_____

_____

Courage and Commitment

 My Choices

- This week I will choose to let go of the familiar and hold on to God's hand.

- This week I will choose to study and meditate on God's Word.

- This week I will choose to teach my children that God is always with them, so they will have the courage to stand up for what is right.

- This week I will choose to: _____

_____

_____

_____

_____

 For Further Reading: Joshua 1–2

Courage is the power to let go
of the familiar.

RAYMOND LINDQUIST

Who Gets the Glory?

 Key Scripture: Judges 7:2–4

The LORD said to Gideon, "You have too many warriors with you. If I let all of you fight the Midianites, the Israelites will boast to me that they saved themselves by their own strength. Therefore, tell the people, 'Whoever is timid or afraid may leave and go home.'" Twenty-two thousand of them went home, leaving only ten thousand who were willing to fight.

But the LORD told Gideon, "There are still too many!"

We are not to think that, where we see no possibility, God sees none.

MARCUS DOD

Who Gets the Glory?

 ## Mom's Reflection

The Supermom Syndrome seems to run rampant in our culture. A supermom does it all. She is the protector of her children, the coordinator of the overloaded family calendar, the provider for all her kids' needs. The supermom believes the livelihood and success of her children depend upon her careful planning, preparation, and follow-through. She is self-sufficient.

God, however, calls us to be God-sufficient. Gideon started out with a superarmy. But God was not looking for an army that could "do it all." He wanted a humble army that would look to him for its success and recognize that victory was found in him alone, not in self-sufficiency. God eventually whittled down Gideon's army to three hundred men. He granted the victory, and the honor went to him.

God isn't looking for supermoms who can do it all on their own. He is looking for moms who will look to him for guidance, wisdom, direction, and strength. If a supermom's kids turn out great, then she gets the glory. But when children are raised by wise and humble moms who depend on God for strength and guidance, then the glory is his.

My Thoughts

Am I depending on God, or am I depending on myself to raise my kids? _____

_____

_____

_____

_____

_____

♡ **My Prayer**

"All-sufficient God, I praise you, for you are all power and all wisdom. I recognize that I'm not a supermom. I can't do it all. I praise you that you can! Thank you for loving and caring for me and my family. Teach me to be responsible, humble, wise, and strong. Help my children to grow up to be well-balanced adults who follow you, so that you may be glorified. Thank you for being the protector of my family and the guardian of each of our souls. In Jesus's name I pray, amen."

This week I'm praying for:_____

_____

_____

_____

_____

_____

Who Gets the Glory?

 My Choices

- This week I will choose to see the God-possibilities instead of my own inabilities.

- This week I will choose to be God-sufficient rather than self-sufficient.

- This week I will choose to give God the glory and not myself.

- This week I will choose to: _____

_____

_____

_____

_____

For Further Reading: Judges 7

God is not waiting to show us strong
in his behalf, but himself
strong in our behalf.
That makes a lot of difference.
He is not out to demonstrate
what we can do but what he can do.

VANCE HAVNER

Rich and Rewarding Loyalty

 Key Scripture: Ruth 1:14–18

*But Ruth insisted on staying with Naomi. "See,"
Naomi said to her, "your sister-in-law has gone
back to her people and to her gods. You should do
the same."*

*But Ruth replied, "Don't ask me to leave you
and turn back. I will go wherever you go and live
wherever you live. Your people will be my people,
and your God will be my God. I will die where
you die and will be buried there. May the LORD
punish me severely if I allow anything but death
to separate us!" So when Naomi saw that Ruth
had made up her mind to go with her, she stopped
urging her.*

We are all in the same boat in a stormy sea,
and we owe each other a terrible loyalty.

G. K. CHESTERTON

Rich and Rewarding Loyalty

 Mom's Reflection

Loyalty is a rare commodity in today's world. When the going gets tough, most people get going. But as we see in this passage, Ruth was not one of those people. Although her husband had just died and she no longer had a family obligation to her mother-in-law, Naomi, she chose to stay with her. Ruth wasn't even an Israelite, yet she pledged to continue following Naomi's God.

Now and then it's healthy for us to do a loyalty self-check. We must ask ourselves, "Am I loyal to the people in my life through my words and actions?" "Do I speak kindly about my husband and my friends behind their backs?" "Am I loyal to my children?"

Perhaps you think that loyalty to our kids is a given. Isn't every mom loyal to her children? But sometimes we forget that kids are people too. Even with our children we must guard against sharing stories or retelling events that would damage their spirits or hurt their feelings. Loyalty was a way of life for Ruth, and the Lord rewarded her for her it. Jesus himself was born from her lineage! Let's be aware of our level of loyalty and ask the Lord to strengthen that quality in us.

Week 8

 ## My Thoughts

How do I show loyalty to my family and friends? Are there any areas of disloyalty in my life that need to be resolved?

_____

_____

_____

_____

_____

_____

My Prayer

"Faithful Father, I praise you for being loyal, trustworthy, and loving toward me. Help me to reflect that same type of loyal love toward the people in my life. Give me the courage and strength to guard my tongue and my actions. Keep me from hurting the ones I love through disloyal words or deeds. Thank you for my children, my family members, and my friends, and help me to honor them with loyalty and faithfulness. In Jesus's name I pray, amen."

This week I'm praying for:_____

_____

_____

_____

_____

Rich and Rewarding Loyalty

☺ My Choices

- This week I will choose to guard my mouth and only speak well of others.

- This week I will choose to do a self-check of my loyalty toward family and friends.

- This week I will choose to teach my children about the richness and rewards of loyalty.

- This week I will choose to: _____

_____

_____

_____

_____

 For Further Reading: The Book of Ruth

There is one element that
is worth its weight in gold and
that is loyalty. It will cover a
multitude of weaknesses.

PHILIP ARMOUR

Delighting in God's Blessings

 Key Scripture: 1 Samuel 1:27–28; 2:1–2

"I asked the LORD to give me this child, and he has given me my request. Now I am giving him to the LORD, and he will belong to the LORD his whole life." And they worshiped the LORD there.

> *Then Hannah prayed:*
> *"My heart rejoices in the LORD!*
> *Oh, how the LORD has blessed me!*
> *Now I have an answer for my enemies,*
> *as I delight in your deliverance.*
> *No one is holy like the LORD!*
> *There is no one besides you;*
> *there is no Rock like our God."*

We should spend as much time in thanking God for his benefits as we spent in asking him for them.

ST. VINCENT DE PAUL

Delighting in God's Blessings

 Mom's Reflection

Oh, the joy of answered prayer! In this passage we see the wonder of God's plan. Hannah, a precious, God-fearing woman, was barren. As each year passed without a pregnancy, her pain and anguish grew. To make matters worse, she was ridiculed by her husband's second wife (of all people) for her inability to conceive.

How could God allow Hannah to suffer so much? It's difficult to understand, and yet, God knew the whole picture. Hannah brought her request for a child before the Lord, and he answered her. Out of her pain and perseverance, she eventually bore a child named Samuel, who grew up to be a faithful servant of God and a leader in Israel.

Hannah's prayer of thanksgiving after the birth of her son is one of joy and delight in God's blessing. As praying moms we, too, can find peace in the asking and joy in the answer. Let's be faithful to offer thanks, glorifying God as we see his plan unfold in our lives. It's easy to pour out our needs to the Lord; thanksgiving and praise don't always flow as vibrantly. Let's take a cue from Hannah and worship the Lord as we request and as we receive.

 **My Thoughts**

Do I worship and thank the Lord as I seek his help and blessing? What can I thank him for this week? _____

_____

_____

_____

_____

_____

♡ **My Prayer**

"Wonderful Lord, I praise you, for you are good and you are powerful. I praise you because you have a plan for my life. I trust your plan. Thank you for all the ways you have already moved and worked on my behalf. You have blessed me so much! Thank you for being my rock and my refuge as I wait on you for the blessings to come. Be glorified in my life! In Jesus's name I pray, amen."

This week I'm praying for:_____

_____

_____

_____

_____

_____

_____

Delighting in God's Blessings

:) My Choices

- This week I will choose to give all my cares, concerns, and requests to God in prayer.
- This week I will choose to spend more time thanking God and delighting in his blessings.
- This week I will choose to teach my children to thank God in their prayers.
- This week I will choose to: _____

_____

_____

_____

_____

 For Further Reading: 1 Samuel 1

He who has learned to pray
has learned the greatest secret
of a holy and happy life.

WILLIAM LAW

God Is Our Provider

 Key Scripture: 2 Kings 4:1–7

One day the widow of one of Elisha's fellow prophets came to Elisha and cried out to him, "My husband who served you is dead, and you know how he feared the LORD. But now a creditor has come, threatening to take my two sons as slaves."

"What can I do to help you?" Elisha asked. "Tell me, what do you have in the house?"

"Nothing at all, except a flask of olive oil," she replied.

And Elisha said, "Borrow as many empty jars as you can from your friends and neighbors. Then go into your house with your sons and shut the door behind you. Pour olive oil from your flask into the jars, setting the jars aside as they are filled."

So she did as she was told. Her sons brought many jars to her, and she filled one after another. Soon every container was full to the brim! . . .

God Is Our Provider

When she told the man of God what had happened, he said to her, "Now sell the olive oil and pay your debts, and there will be enough money left over to support you and your sons."

 Mom's Reflection

What a blessed picture of God's tender care for his people! The poor widow had nothing in her house—only a single flask of olive oil (used for cooking, for lamps, and for fuel). Because she had a faithful and obedient heart, however, God took what little she had to offer and blessed her faithful obedience with overflowing abundance. Think of the testimony this was to her sons! No doubt they were thinking, "If only we had gone out to find more jars!"

As mothers we can glean many wonderful truths from this short story. We are comforted to see God's care for this God-fearing household—and reminded that the Lord is our provider too. We're also reminded that faith in God's provision doesn't mean that we can sit back and do nothing, expecting blessings to fall from the sky. The widow asked Elisha for help, then she faithfully and obediently did as she was told. We, too, are called to be responsible and obedient to God's direction.

Finally, we can draw encouragement from the way that God took what little this woman had and multiplied it abundantly. We may think we have little to offer. But God can take our simple love, faith, and obedience and multiply it into significant blessing for our homes.

Week 10

 My Thoughts

Do I look to God as my provider day to day? Can others see
my trust in him? _____

_____

_____

_____

_____

_____

My Prayer

"Wonderful Lord and Perfect Provider, I praise you for your
tender love and care for me. I praise you for your magnificent
power that is able to take what little I have to offer and use
it in a wonderful way. Thank you for looking after the needs
of my family. Help me to live in faithful obedience to you.
In Jesus's name I pray, amen."

This week I'm praying for:_____

_____

_____

_____

_____

_____

_____

_____

God Is Our Provider

 **My Choices**

- This week I will choose to look to God as my provider.

- This week I will choose to faithfully obey what he leads me to do.

- This week I will choose to teach my children about God's faithfulness.

- This week I will choose to: _____

_____

_____

_____

_____

 For Further Reading: 2 Kings 4–5

Faith is a living, daring confidence in
God's grace, so sure and
certain that a man could stake
his life on it a thousand times.

MARTIN LUTHER

The Battle Is the Lord's

 Key Scripture: 2 Chronicles 20:13–17

As all the men of Judah stood before the LORD with their little ones, wives, and children, the Spirit of the LORD came upon one of the men standing there. . . . He said, "Listen, King Jehoshaphat! Listen, all you people of Judah and Jerusalem! This is what the LORD says: Do not be afraid! Don't be discouraged by this mighty army, for the battle is not yours, but God's. Tomorrow, march out against them. You will find them coming up through the ascent of Ziz at the end of the valley that opens into the wilderness of Jeruel. But you will not even need to fight. Take your positions; then stand still and watch the LORD's victory. He is with you, O people of Judah and Jerusalem. Do not be afraid or discouraged. Go out there tomorrow, for the LORD is with you!"

The Battle Is the Lord's

 **Mom's Reflection**

What battles are you facing? You probably don't have a large army lined up against you, but I'm guessing you have some battles in your life. We all do. For some of us it's a battle with a particular fear or worry. For others it's a battle with a particular relationship or potty training or a strong-willed child. For still others it's a battle with food or alcohol or prescription drugs.

It's easy to think that we're in the battle alone, and the victory is up to us. But in this Bible passage we read the words, "Do not be afraid! Don't be discouraged by this mighty army, for the battle is not yours, but God's." Dear sweet, fellow mom, are you willing to give the battle over to God and stop trying to fight it on your own? Are you willing to courageously stand against temptation and ask the Lord to do a mighty work? Stand firm, be courageous, listen to the Lord's instructions, and obey. Trust him to give you strength!

Later, in 2 Chronicles 20, we read that the Israelites went out the next morning, took their stand, and faced the enemy. And God brought the victory! King Jehoshaphat declared a statement that we, as moms, need to remember as we face our own battles: "Believe in the LORD your God, and you will be able to stand firm" (verse 20).

My Thoughts

What battle am I facing? Am I willing to seek the Lord's help for victory? _____

_____

_____

_____

_____

_____

My Prayer

"High King of heaven, I praise you, for you are able to bring victory in my life. You have all the power I need to defeat my enemies! Help me to have the faith and courage to believe and stand firm. Lord, I give all my battles to you. I know I cannot win in my own strength; I need you. Help me to do my part. Thank you for always being with me. In Jesus's name I pray, amen."

This week I'm praying for:_____

_____

_____

_____

_____

_____

_____

The Battle Is the Lord's

☺ My Choices

- This week I will choose to give my battles to the Lord.
- This week I will choose to stand firm in my faith.
- This week I will choose to cast away fear and discouragement, knowing that the Lord is with me.
- This week I will choose to: _____

_____

_____

_____

_____

_____

 For Further Reading: 2 Chronicles 20;
Ephesians 6:10–18

When distress and cares oppress you,
And you seem to walk alone;
Look up, friend, for
God will bless you,
"He is mindful of His own."

AUTHOR UNKNOWN

God's Glorious Restoration

 Key Scripture: Ezra 9:8–9

But now we have been given a brief moment of grace, for the LORD our God has allowed a few of us to survive as a remnant. He has given us security in this holy place. Our God has brightened our eyes and granted us some relief from our slavery. For we were slaves, but in his unfailing love our God did not abandon us in our slavery. Instead, he caused the kings of Persia to treat us favorably. He revived us so that we were able to rebuild the Temple of our God and repair its ruins. He has given us a protective wall in Judah and Jerusalem.

J esus came not only to teach but to save, not only to reveal God to mankind, but also to redeem mankind for God.

JOHN R. W. STOTT

God's Glorious Restoration

 Mom's Reflection

Have you ever lost hope? Have you ever come to a point where you thought the circumstances or relationships in your life were so broken, they could never be restored? Surely that's the way the people of Israel felt when Jerusalem and the Temple were destroyed in 586 BC and they were taken as exiles to Babylon. There seemed to be no hope for restoration of their Temple or their nation. But God made a way. Over a period of many years, he worked in the lives of some of his faithful servants and in the heart of the king of Persia. Eventually, the people were allowed to return to Jerusalem to rebuild the Temple—and their hope was restored in the process.

Our God is a redeeming, restoring God. He may not restore your situation in the exact way or along the same timetable you would have planned, but you can take hope in his mighty power and perfect work. He is able to restore relationships. He is able to restore circumstances. He is able to redeem lives.

Without a doubt, the greatest redemption of all took place when the Lord delivered us from the slavery of sin and restored us to a right relationship with him through the sacrifice of his Son, Jesus. I love how Ezra says, "Our God has brightened our eyes." Let's rejoice in God's redemption of our souls. And may our bright eyes reflect the bright hope we have in him!

My Thoughts

In what ways have I seen God's redeeming work in my life? In what areas do I need to trust His redemptive work?

_____

_____

_____

_____

_____

My Prayer

"Redeeming Lord and wonderful Father, I praise you, because you have redeemed my life from the pit and crowned me with loving-kindness and tender mercies. Thank you for the hope I have in you! You are the one I trust to bring restoration to my broken circumstances. I know the plan you have for my life is far bigger than I can see. Give me strength and patience to wait for your perfect work. In Jesus's name I pray, amen."

This week I'm praying for:_____

_____

_____

_____

_____

_____

God's Glorious Restoration

🙂 My Choices

- This week I will choose to place my hope in my loving heavenly Father.
- This week I will choose to stop focusing on my problems.
- This week I will choose to pray for God's restoration and redemption in my circumstances.
- This week I will choose to: _____

_____

_____

_____

_____

_____

 For Further Reading: Psalm 103

> Hope, child, tomorrow and tomorrow
> still, and every tomorrow hope;
> trust while you live. Hope, each time
> the dawn doth heaven fill, be there to
> ask as God is there to give.
>
> VICTOR HUGO

Big Task, Big Testimony

Key Scripture: Nehemiah 2:4–6; 6:15–16

The king asked, "Well, how can I help you?"

With a prayer to the God of heaven, I replied, "If it please Your Majesty and if you are pleased with me, your servant, send me to Judah to rebuild the city where my ancestors are buried."

The king, with the queen sitting beside him, asked, "How long will you be gone? When will you return?" So the king agreed, and I set a date for my departure. . . .

So on October 2 the wall was finally finished— just fifty-two days after we had begun. When our enemies and the surrounding nations heard about it, they were frightened and humiliated. They realized that this work had been done with the help of our God.

Big Task, Big Testimony

 Mom's Reflection

"I just can't handle it!" I'm guessing you've said these words at some point in your life. I know I have. Perhaps it was when you brought home your first baby. Maybe it was when you agreed to teach the third grade Sunday school class or when you started a new job. Whatever it was, it seemed like a huge task, and you knew you were about to step way out of your comfort zone.

When Nehemiah became concerned because the walls of Jerusalem were in disrepair, he didn't sit around and complain about it; he took action. He knew the task was too big for one man. But he also knew that God would use his gifts and talents to motivate others and get the monumental task done. In that process, Nehemiah faced insults, threats, and sabotage from his enemies. Yet when his fellow workers became fearful, Nehemiah prayed, encouraged them, and found a way to keep moving forward. What was the end result? God was glorified, because everyone knew the job was too big to be done without God's help.

As moms we are going to find ourselves in situations bigger than our capabilities. It's inevitable. When that happens we have a choice. We can choose to whine and complain in self-pity; or, as Nehemiah did, we can choose to look to God for help, move forward in his strength—and give him all the glory!

My Thoughts

When I'm in a situation that seems too big to handle, do I ask God for help and trust him to help me?

_____

_____

_____

_____

_____

_____

My Prayer

"Mighty God and Holy Father, I praise you for the guidance and ability you give me to handle the tasks you have set before me. When I feel overwhelmed, please grant me your strength. When I feel inadequate, please give me what I need for the moment. I look to you and trust you for help. May you be glorified in everything you do in and through my life. In Jesus's name I pray, amen."

This week I'm praying for:_____

_____

_____

_____

_____

_____

Big Task, Big Testimony

☺ My Choices

- This week I will choose to ask God for help and guidance each day.

- This week I will choose to look for what God can do through my abilities and talents.

- This week I will choose to take positive action instead of complain.

- This week I will choose to: _____

_____

_____

_____

_____

 For Further Reading: Nehemiah 8

The only difference between
stumbling blocks and steppingstones
is the way you use them.

AUTHOR UNKNOWN

Out of the Comfort Zone

 Key Scripture: Esther 4:13–16

Mordecai sent back this reply to Esther: "Don't think for a moment that you will escape there in the palace when all other Jews are killed. If you keep quiet at a time like this, deliverance for the Jews will arise from some other place, but you and your relatives will die. What's more, who can say but that you have been elevated to the palace for just such a time as this?"

Then Esther sent this reply to Mordecai: "Go and gather together all the Jews of Susa and fast for me. Do not eat or drink for three days, night or day. My maids and I will do the same. And then, though it is against the law, I will go in to see the king. If I must die, I am willing to die."

God's ways are behind the scenes, but He moves all the scenes which He is behind.

JOHN NELSON DARBY

Out of the Comfort Zone

 Mom's Reflection

When God placed Esther in a place of honor—as queen in a Persian palace—she was a long way from her humble beginnings as a young Jewish girl. But God had a plan for her life that was bigger than simply living in royal comfort. After a decree to destroy the Jews was unwittingly signed by the king, she chose to step out of her comfort zone and take a risk on behalf of her people.

As Esther walked into unknown territory, there was one thing she knew for sure: she must depend on God. She fasted and prayed, and she asked others to fast and pray for her. She knew that she couldn't rely on the comfort of her position; she had to rely on the comfort of God's power and sovereignty.

Wouldn't it be nice to live in a comfy, safe situation with all of our ducks neatly in a row? Unfortunately, that's not usually how life plays out. As moms we all have times when we are stretched by our circumstances or challenged to step out of our comfort zones. When that happens we can take a lesson from Esther: Trust in God's sovereignty, pray for his help, and make a wise plan of action. Only God has the power to bring us safely through.

My Thoughts

In what ways have I been pushed out of my comfort zone? Do I tend to trust God in the stretching times? _____

_____

_____

_____

_____

_____

My Prayer

"Sovereign Lord, I praise you, because you have plans for my life that are far bigger than I know. Thank you that no matter what I go through, you are with me. No matter where I am, you are there. In the nice, comfy times and in the stretching, scary times, you never leave me. Please grant me strength and wisdom to walk the path that you have set before me, and bring me safely to the other side. In Jesus's name I pray, amen."

This week I'm praying for:_____

_____

_____

_____

_____

_____

Out of the Comfort Zone

 **My Choices**

- This week I will choose to trust God's sovereign plan for my life and my kids' lives.

- This week I will choose to accept the fact that I may be pulled out of my comfort zone.

- This week I will choose to pray for wisdom for the steps I am to take.

- This week I will choose to: _____

_____

_____

_____

_____

_____

 For Further Reading: The Book of Esther

> Appearances can be deceptive.
> The fact that we cannot see what
> God is doing does not mean
> that he is doing nothing.
>
> SINCLAIR FERGUSON

Trusting God

 Key Scripture: Job 2:8–10

Then Job scraped his skin with a piece of broken pottery as he sat among the ashes. His wife said to him, "Are you still trying to maintain your integrity? Curse God and die."

But Job replied, "You talk like a godless woman. Should we accept only good things from the hand of God and never anything bad?" So in all this, Job said nothing wrong.

God's goodness is the preeminent expression of his glory.

JERRY BRIDGES

Trusting God

 Mom's Reflection

The trials of Job: I'm sure you're at least somewhat familiar with his story. A godly man, Job was tested by Satan (with God's permission). All of his possessions were destroyed; his children were taken; not even his health was spared. To make matters worse, he had to deal with accusing friends and a negative wife. Through it all, Job questioned God, but he did not curse God. His faith was shaken but not destroyed.

When terrible things happen in our lives, it's easy to think, *Hey, wait a minute. I've been pretty good. Why is God doing this to me?* But one of the powerful lessons we learn from Job is that we cannot understand God's ways. His plan is way beyond our comprehension. God is the sovereign Lord of the universe—and we are not.

A second lesson is that acceptance is the first step toward trusting God in our difficulties. We may not like our situation, but we can say with Job, "Should we accept only good things from the hand of God and never anything bad?" Job's faith in God, not his understanding, is what carried him through all his troubles. Our faith in God will carry us through as well.

My Thoughts

In what areas of my life do I have to relinquish my need to understand God and simply trust him? _____

_____

_____

_____

_____

_____

_____

♡ My Prayer

"Mighty God, I stand in awe of your majesty and power. You are a good God! Although my comprehension is weak, I trust in your goodness. Thank you that you have a plan that goes far beyond what I can see; thank you that you care about my deepest longings and needs. Thank you that you are with me in my pain as well as my joy. Help me to be aware of your presence. In Jesus's name I pray, amen."

This week I'm praying for: _____

_____

_____

_____

_____

_____

Trusting God

 **My Choices**

- This week I will choose to place my faith and trust in the sovereignty of God.

- This week I will choose to accept the things I cannot change.

- This week I will choose to relinquish my right to understand why.

- This week I will choose to: _____

_____

_____

_____

_____

_____

 For Further Reading: Job 1–2; 42

High in the heavens, eternal God,
Thy goodness in full glory shines;
Thy truth shall break through every cloud
That veils and darkens thy designs.

Isaac Watts

Delighting in the Lord

 Key Scripture: Psalm 37:3–5

Trust in the LORD and do good.
Then you will live safely in the land and
prosper.
Take delight in the LORD,
and he will give you your heart's desires.
Commit everything you do to the LORD.
Trust him, and he will help you.

Seek his will in all you do, and he will
direct your paths.

SOLOMON

Delighting in the Lord

 ## Mom's Reflection

There are days when my head is swimming with too many details: the grocery list, the laundry pile, the phone calls to return—and don't even get me started on all the emails that have stacked up! Perhaps you feel the same way. Your to-do list may be a little different, but your brain is swirling with minutia just the same. The practical side of us says, "Just make a list of what needs to be done and then do it." The Lord says, "Commit your work to me and I will help you."

As we commit each day to the Lord through prayer, he helps us order our steps. Some things are necessary and some things can wait, and we need his guidance and discernment to know the difference. As we lay even the smallest details of our day before the Lord, he directs our path

What a wonderful God! It's not hard to delight in such a God—to find our enjoyment in knowing him. As moms we can delight in his presence all day long. What a beautiful way to walk through the day, devoting our tasks to him!

 **My Thoughts**

What details or to-dos do I need to commit to the Lord today? _____

_____

_____

_____

_____

_____

My Prayer

"I praise you, God most high, maker of heaven and earth. You know the path I need to take. You know the way that is best for me to go. I look to you for guidance and direction. I give you my list of today's to-dos. Show me what is necessary and what is not. Help me to be wise. Most importantly, help me to delight in you and trust you in everything I do. In Jesus's name I pray, amen."

This week I'm praying for:_____

_____

_____

_____

_____

_____

_____

Delighting in the Lord

 My Choices

- This week I will choose to commit my work to the Lord.

- This week I will choose to seek his guidance and delight in his presence all day long.

- This week I will choose to teach my kids the blessings that come from delighting in the Lord and committing their ways to him.

- This week I will choose to: _____

_____

_____

_____

_____

_____

 For Further Reading: Psalm 37

> It is comforting to know that not only the steps but also the stops of a good man are ordered by the Lord.
>
> GEORGE MUELLER

The Power of Our Words

 Key Scripture: Proverbs 15:1–4; 18:4, 20

A gentle answer turns away wrath, but harsh words stir up anger.

The wise person makes learning a joy; fools spout only foolishness.

The LORD is watching everywhere, keeping his eye on both the evil and the good.

Gentle words bring life and health; a deceitful tongue crushes the spirit. . . .

A person's words can be life-giving water; words of true wisdom are as refreshing as a bubbling brook. . . .

Words satisfy the soul as food satisfies the stomach; the right words on a person's lips bring satisfaction.

Kindness is a grace that all can understand.

J. C. RYLE

The Power of Our Words

 Mom's Reflection

Like it or not, our words are powerful. They can be a life-giving spring that pours out wisdom and encouragement; they can also be a tool that stirs the pot of anger and dissatisfaction. As moms we want to consider not only what we say, but how we say it. After all, isn't that what we tell our kids to do? They need to learn from our example. They need to hear what strong but gentle words sound like.

The most effective discipline is not delivered through shouts and screams, but rather through caring, guarded, and thoughtful instruction. In the very last chapter of Proverbs, Solomon describes "the wife of noble character" this way: "When she speaks, her words are wise, and kindness is the rule when she gives instructions" (Proverbs 31:26). As we teach, train, and discipline our children, let's never underestimate the power of wise, kind, and well-chosen words.

Week 17

 ## My Thoughts

Are there any changes I need to make in the way I communicate with my family? _____

_____

_____

_____

_____

_____

My Prayer

"Loving and kind heavenly Father, I praise you for your wisdom and power. You alone are the Lord. Thank you for your kindness and gentleness toward me. Lead me to speak kind and gentle words to my children in a spirit of calm. Give me self-control when I'm angry, so that I do not hurt my children or others with my words. Help me to use only life-giving words when I speak to my family and friends. In Jesus's name I pray, amen."

This week I'm praying for:_____

_____

_____

_____

_____

_____

The Power of Our Words

 **My Choices**

- This week I will choose to use only life-giving words with my family and friends.

- This week I will choose to discipline my children with strong but gentle instruction.

- This week I will choose to allow the law of kindness to rule my tongue.

- This week I will choose to: _____

_____

_____

_____

_____

_____

 For Further Reading: James 3

The one who has wisdom
in his head and heart does
not need to shout at others.

SPIROS ZODHIATES

A Time and a Season

 Key Scripture: Ecclesiastes 3:1–8

There is a time for everything,
a season for every activity under heaven.
A time to be born and a time to die.
A time to plant and a time to harvest.
A time to kill and a time to heal.
A time to tear down and a time to rebuild.
A time to cry and a time to laugh.
A time to grieve and a time to dance.
A time to scatter stones and a time to gather stones.
A time to embrace and a time to turn away.
A time to search and a time to lose.
A time to keep and a time to throw away.
A time to tear and a time to mend.
A time to be quiet and a time to speak up.
A time to love and a time to hate.
A time for war and a time for peace.

A Time and a Season

 Mom's Reflection

"A time for everything" seems like a simple concept. But it's not so simple when it comes to the family calendar. It's amazing how quickly we fill up our time with so many different activities. It is almost as if we believe that we must do everything, and we must do it now! Why do we let ourselves get so busy? Maybe we're afraid our kids will be left out or fall behind if we don't sign them up for certain sports or activities. Maybe we commit ourselves to certain things just because we're asked to, and we don't like to say no.

Wisdom tells us that we don't need to do everything right now. There is a time and a season for everything! So instead of automatically signing the kids up for art lessons, T-ball, gymnastics, and Scouts, let's slow down and rethink our schedules. Let's take a deliberate look at what is necessary and prudent and learn to say no. Let's change the pace of life from doing everything all at once to doing the right things at the right time. Let's ask the Lord what he would have us do this year and save the rest for another time.

My Thoughts

Is there anything in my family's activities or my personal schedule that needs to change? _____

_____

_____

_____

_____

_____

My Prayer

"Wise and loving shepherd of my soul, I praise you for the way you care for me. Thank you for taking an interest in the details of my life and the lives of each of my family members. Please give me wisdom to know what my family and I should do with our time. Help me to recognize the season we are in and the activities that are necessary and appropriate. Guide us in the right direction, so we can glorify you in all that we do. In Jesus's name I pray, amen."

This week I'm praying for:_____

_____

_____

_____

_____

_____

A Time and a Season

 My Choices

- This week I will choose to take a deliberate look at my family's schedule of activities.

- This week I will choose to pray for direction in how we use our time.

- This week I will choose to use my time wisely each day.

- This week I will choose to: _____

_____

_____

_____

_____

_____

 For Further Reading: Psalm 90

Taking first things first . . . often
reduces the most complex
human problem to
a manageable proportion.

DWIGHT D. EISENHOWER

Beautiful Passion

 Key Scripture: Song of Songs 1:15–17

Young Man: "How beautiful you are, my beloved, how beautiful! Your eyes are soft like doves."
Young Woman: "What a lovely, pleasant sight you are, my love, as we lie here on the grass, shaded by cedar trees and spreading firs."

The first sexual thought in the universe was God's, not man's.

DOUG BARNETT

Beautiful Passion

 Mom's Reflection

Sizzling! That's how I would define the romance between the lovers in Song of Songs. Their words drip with love and admiration for one another. Each one's only desire is to bring the other pleasure. As they express their feelings and longings, their dialogue offers a beautiful picture of marital love and passion. Ultimately, their hearts and souls are joined together not just through words, but through the physical expression of their love.

Sex within the bonds of marriage is a pleasure and a delight. God designed sex to be a wonderful and intimate connection between a husband and wife. Sadly, the media portrays sex as a casual, no-strings-attached activity—a widespread misconception that inevitably leads to more heartache than happiness. As positive Christian women let's enjoy sex as God truly meant it to be—a beautiful bonding, both physically and emotionally, between a man and a woman who have committed themselves to one another for life through marriage. What pleasure!

My Thoughts

What do I really admire about my husband? How can I show him my love and admiration more fully? _____

_____

_____

_____

_____

_____

My Prayer

"Most Holy God, I praise you for your pure and holy love toward me! Thank you for showing me what true love looks like. Thank you for creating sex to be a beautiful connection between my husband and me. Show me how to bring delight and pleasure to my husband. Help me to express my respect and admiration for him. May we grow closer to one another as, together, we grow closer to you. In Jesus's name I pray, amen."

This week I'm praying for:_____

_____

_____

_____

_____

_____

Beautiful Passion

 My Choices

- This week I will choose to let my husband know how much I love and admire him.

- This week I will choose to enjoy my husband physically.

- This week I will choose to encourage greater intimacy with my husband.

- This week I will choose to: _____

_____

_____

_____

_____

For Further Reading: The Song of Songs

> The powerful sexual drives which are built into man's relationship with woman are not seen in Scripture as the foundation of marriage, but the consummation and physical expression of it.
>
> SINCLAIR FERGUSON

His Glorious Strength

 Key Scripture: Isaiah 40:27–31

*O Israel, how can you say the LORD does not see
your troubles? How can you say God refuses to hear
your case? Have you never heard or understood?
Don't you know that the LORD is the everlasting
God, the Creator of all the earth? He never grows
faint or weary. No one can measure the depths of
his understanding. He gives power to those who
are tired and worn out; he offers strength to the
weak. Even youths will become exhausted, and
young men will give up. But those who wait on
the LORD will find new strength. They will fly high
on wings like eagles. They will run and not grow
weary. They will walk and not faint.*

Lord, how happy it is when strong
afflictions from Thee raise in us strong
affections for Thee!

FRANCIS BURKITT

His Glorious Strength

 ## Mom's Reflection

Worn out? Exhausted? Feel like you can't go on? Join the club! Thankfully, the Lord sees and understands our situation. As the everlasting God and Creator of all the earth, he never grows tired and weary—we do, but he doesn't. That means we can lean on him for strength at any time. What greater comfort can there be than to know that our wonderful, strong God sees our troubles, understands our weaknesses, and wants to be our strength?

In this passage in Isaiah, we see that those who wait on the Lord gain new strength. How do we, as busy moms, wait on the Lord? Waiting on the Lord doesn't mean that we sit back, twiddle our thumbs, and give up our responsibilities because "God will do it all." No, it means that we confidently and patiently trust God in the midst of our responsibilities, knowing that he will help us. It means believing that as we keep our eyes on him, he will give us new strength to complete the tasks set before us. With his great power undergirding us, we *will* run and not grow weary; we will walk and not faint!

 **My Thoughts**

How do I presently lean on God? In what ways do I need to trust him? _____

_____

_____

_____

_____

_____

_____

♡ My Prayer

"Glorious God, wonderful Father, I praise you for being my strength, my rock, and my refuge. I praise you for seeing my whole situation and understanding better than anyone what I'm going through. Thank you for offering your strength to me. Thank you that you never grow tired or weary. Help me to wait on you with expectation, knowing that you will give me what I need for the journey you've set before me."

This week I'm praying for:_____

_____

_____

_____

_____

_____

His Glorious Strength

:) My Choices

- This week I will choose to remember that God sees my troubles and understands my situation.

- This week I will choose to confidently trust his work in my life.

- This week I will choose to look to God for strength.

- This week I will choose to: _____

_____

_____

_____

_____

_____

For Further Reading: Isaiah 40; 43

God hath in himself all power to
defend you, all wisdom to direct you,
all mercy to pardon you, all grace to
enrich you, all righteousness to clothe
you, all goodness to supply you, and
all happiness to crown you.

THOMAS BROOKS

God's Perfect Plan

 Key Scripture: Jeremiah 29:10–14

"The truth is that you will be in Babylon for seventy years. But then I will come and do for you all the good things I have promised, and I will bring you home again. For I know the plans I have for you," says the LORD. "They are plans for good and not for disaster, to give you a future and a hope. In those days when you pray, I will listen. If you look for me in earnest, you will find me when you seek me. I will be found by you," says the LORD. "I will end your captivity and restore your fortunes. I will gather you out of the nations where I sent you and bring you home again to your own land."

O Lord, help me not to despise or oppose what I do not understand.

WILLIAM PENN

God's Perfect Plan

 ## Mom's Reflection

In this passage we see the Lord's reassurance to his people. Yes, they were going to go through captivity, but God wanted them to know that he would hear their prayers. He wanted them to know that, despite difficult circumstances and all appearances to the contrary, he still had a great plan for their lives.

We all need reassurance at times, don't we? Whether we're going through a long-term challenge or a short-term frustration, there is tremendous comfort in knowing that God has a bigger plan—and a good plan—in mind. I'm sure the Israelites were thinking that seventy years in captivity was not a good plan, but God reassured them that he would give them a future and a hope. He let them know he intended to restore their fortunes and bring them back to their own land.

We have the same assurance. Not only does God have a plan for us, but it's a good plan. What's more, God promises to listen to our prayers. When we seek him, we will find him. What a powerful message for us and for our families!

My Thoughts

In what ways do I see God's plan at work in my life? Am I willing to trust that plan, whatever my circumstances?

_____

_____

_____

_____

_____

_____

My Prayer

"Powerful God, I praise you, because you have a good plan for my life. I praise you, because you are able to carry out that plan in your time and in your way. I trust your love for me. Thank you for hearing my prayers. Thank you for the way you work in my life far beyond what I can see. Help me to continue to seek you all the days of my life. In Jesus's name I pray, amen."

This week I'm praying for:_____

_____

_____

_____

_____

_____

God's Perfect Plan

☺ My Choices

- This week I will choose to rejoice in the fact that God has a plan for my life.

- This week I will choose to rejoice in the fact that God has a plan for my children's lives.

- This week I will choose to rest in the fact that God's plan is a good plan.

- This week I will choose: _____

_____

_____

_____

_____

 For Further Reading: Jeremiah 29–31

Nothing whatever surprises God;
all things that happen are
absolutely certain from all eternity
because they are all embraced
in God's eternal plan.

J. GRESHAM MACHEN

Great Is His Faithfulness!

 Key Scripture: Lamentations 3:17–26

Peace has been stripped away, and I have forgotten what prosperity is. I cry out, "My splendor is gone! Everything I had hoped for from the LORD is lost!"

The thought of my suffering and homelessness is bitter beyond words. I will never forget this awful time, as I grieve over my loss. Yet I still dare to hope when I remember this:

The unfailing love of the LORD never ends! By his mercies we have been kept from complete destruction. Great is his faithfulness; his mercies begin afresh each day. I say to myself, "The LORD is my inheritance; therefore, I will hope in him!"

The LORD is wonderfully good to those who wait for him and seek him. So it is good to wait quietly for salvation from the LORD.

God smothers repenting sinners in forgiving and redemptive love.

ALBERT N. MARTIN

Great Is His Faithfulness!

 Mom's Reflection

Life was the pits for Jeremiah, the author of Lamentations. Known as "the weeping prophet," he shed many tears over the destruction of Jerusalem and the demise of his nation. Lamentations is not a happy book; yet in the midst of its sadness and despair, we are able to see the shining light of God's redemption. As Jeremiah understood, God's compassion and mercy are ever-present, even when his people are undeserving.

What is causing your grief or heartache? Perhaps your life circumstances seem dismal. Maybe you have experienced the pain of illness or the loss of a loved one. You may grieve over your sin or the poor life choices of one of your family members. Whatever the situation, you can always find a bright ray of hope in the form of God's great faithfulness and unfailing compassion toward his people. His faithfulness and love are bigger than your grief or pain. Run to his open arms, for he is "wonderfully good to those who wait for him and seek him."

Week 22

 My Thoughts

What pain am I holding on to? Am I willing to turn my eyes toward the One who can bring healing from suffering?

_____

_____

_____

_____

_____

Prayer

"Faithful and holy God, all praise and honor belong to you! I praise you for your righteousness, your goodness, and your mercy. Thank you that I can depend on your faithfulness and compassion toward me. Thank you that your mercies are new every morning. Although I grieve over my sin and suffering, I can rejoice in your love and forgiveness. Help me to reflect your loving compassion toward my children, my family members, and others. In Jesus's name I pray, amen."

This week I'm praying for:_____

_____

_____

_____

_____

_____

Great Is His Faithfulness!

 My Choices

- This week I will choose to focus on God's faithfulness and love.

- This week I will choose to repent and turn from any sin or pain I am harboring in my life.

- This week I will choose to continually thank the Lord for his tender mercy.

- This week I will choose to: _____

_____

_____

_____

_____

_____

For Further Reading: Lamentations 3

Immortal love, forever full,
forever flowing free, forever shared,
forever whole,
a never-ebbing sea!

JOHN GREENLEAF WHITTIER

A Beautiful, New Heart

 Key Scripture: Ezekiel 36:26–27

I will give you a new heart with new and right desires, and I will put a new spirit in you. I will take out your stony heart of sin and give you a new, obedient heart. And I will put my Spirit in you so you will obey my laws and do whatever I command.

God regenerates the soul by uniting it to Jesus Christ.

AUGUSTUS H. STRONG

A Beautiful, New Heart

 Mom's Reflection

"Mommy, can I start over?"

Perhaps you heard those words a time or two as your child worked to create a picture. You supplied a fresh piece of paper to let him begin again—and most likely, a huge grin appeared on his eager face.

There's nothing like a clean slate! A fresh start offers new possibilities and opportunities to do things differently. When we came to know Christ through faith, he made all things new in our hearts. He gave us a fresh canvas and began painting a new picture by the power of his Holy Spirit within us. He gave us a fresh start!

Of course, we cannot redo ourselves; only God can. He is the one who transforms our hearts and makes us new creations. Aren't you thankful that God is a God of new beginnings? No matter how bad our lives were before we knew Christ, God gave us a new and fresh start through faith in his Son, Jesus. And he continues to be a God of fresh starts. Through the power of his Holy Spirit, he is ever working to transform our stony hearts of sin into gentle hearts of obedience toward him.

My Thoughts

Have I experienced a changed heart through the redemptive work of Jesus? How does the Holy Spirit work in my life to lead me to obedience? _____

_____

_____

_____

_____

_____

My Prayer

"O Sovereign Lord, I praise you for being my light and my salvation! You are the One who makes all things new. Thank you for your Son, Jesus, who gave his life for me. Thank you that through my faith in him, I can have a new heart and a fresh start. Thank you, too, for your Holy Spirit, who leads me toward obedience. I rejoice in your work in my life! Help me to honor you in all I do. In Jesus's name I pray, amen."

This week I'm praying for:_____

_____

_____

_____

_____

_____

A Beautiful, New Heart

 **My Choices**

- This week I will choose to trust Christ to transform my life.

- This week I will choose to rejoice in my salvation and the newness that it brings.

- This week I will choose to thank God for the work of his Holy Spirit.

- This week I will choose to: _____

_____

_____

_____

_____

_____

 For Further Reading: 2 Corinthians 5:17–21; Psalm 51:10–13

Man's need can only be met by a new creation.

GEOFFREY B. WILSON

A Life That Points to God

 Key Scripture: Daniel 6:25–28

Then King Darius sent this message to the people of every race and nation and language throughout the world:

"Peace and prosperity to you!

"I decree that everyone throughout my kingdom should tremble with fear before the God of Daniel.

> *For he is the living God,*
> *and he will endure forever.*
> *His kingdom will never be destroyed,*
> *and his rule will never end.*
> *He rescues and saves his people;*
> *he performs miraculous signs and*
> *wonders in the heavens and on earth.*
> *He has rescued Daniel*
> *from the power of the lions."*

So Daniel prospered during the reign of Darius and the reign of Cyrus the Persian.

A Life That Points to God

 Mom's Reflection

Daniel was courageous, wise, righteous, and godly. He stood by his convictions, and he lived his life in a way that pointed others to God. What was his secret? Simply put, his faith was not in himself but in the great and mighty God of heaven and earth. Daniel is a hero of the faith because his life served as a testimony to God's majesty and power. Isn't that what we want our own lives to do? More importantly, isn't that the kind of life we want for our children?

Just as Daniel had a sure and strong faith in the one true God, so we want to encourage that kind of faith in our kids. How? We begin by living our own lives of devotion to God, as models for our children to see. We continue by repeating the stories and truths of God's faithfulness over and over again, wherever and whenever we can.

The greatest truth we can pass on to our sons and daughters is to love the Lord their God with all their heart, mind, soul, and strength. If we can teach them that, with God's help, we can raise another generation of faith-filled heroes!

My Thoughts

How do my actions and words point others to Christ?

_____

_____

_____

_____

_____

_____

My Prayer

"Great and glorious God, I praise you for your power and majesty! I praise you for the powerful way you worked in Daniel's life, and I thank you for the powerful way you are working in my life. Thank you for Daniel's example of faith and courage. Help me to teach biblical truths to my kids, so they, like Daniel, will stand firmly for you in their own day and culture. Grant me wisdom and direction in my example and teaching. In Jesus's name I pray, amen."

This week I'm praying for:_____

_____

_____

_____

_____

_____

A Life That Points to God

 **My Choices**

- This week I will choose to live out my faith through my example.

- This week I will choose to tell my kids about God's faithfulness in my life.

- This week I will choose to read stories from God's Word to encourage and build my children's faith.

- This week I will choose to: _____

_____

_____

_____

_____

 For Further Reading: Daniel 6; Deuteronomy 6:4–13

It is faith among men that holds the
moral elements of society together,
as it is faith in God that binds
the world to his throne.

WILLIAM M. EVARTS

Love beyond Limits

 Key Scripture: Hosea 14:8–9

"O Israel, stay away from idols! I am the one who looks after you and cares for you. I am like a tree that is always green, giving my fruit to you all though the year."

Let those who are wise understand these things. Let those who are discerning listen carefully. The paths of the LORD are true and right, and righteous people live by walking in them. But sinners stumble and fall along the way.

The true measure of God's love is that he loves without measure.

AUTHOR UNKNOWN

Love beyond Limits

 ## Mom's Reflection

The book of Hosea is a beautiful portrait of God's redeeming love for his beloved people, despite their faithlessness. The Israelites were guilty of following after other gods, yet the Lord continued to woo them back to himself. It's easy for us to shake our heads and say, "How could the people have failed to recognize the true, faithful, and genuine love of the Lord their God?" We need to ask ourselves the same question. How easy it is for us to try to quench our thirst for love or heal the hurt of our emotional pain by walking in paths that lead away from God!

Hosea's message is clear: "The paths of the LORD are true and right, and righteous people live by walking in them." Let's relish God's true and genuine love for us in every area of our lives. His pure love beckons us to follow him and walk in faithful obedience to his Word. May we hear his voice of love and grace calling, "I am the one who looks after you and cares for you."

🔅 My Thoughts

How does God's love motivate me to live a righteous life?

_____

_____

_____

_____

_____

_____

💟 My Prayer

"Gracious and loving heavenly Father, I praise you, because your love is faithful, satisfying, and sincere. There is no greater love! Thank you for lavishing your love on me, despite my sin and ignorance. Thank you that through Christ you have forgiven me. Help me to recognize your love and draw close to you in faithful obedience. Give me wisdom and discernment so that I might walk in your true and right paths. In Jesus's name I pray, amen."

This week I'm praying for:_____

_____

_____

_____

_____

_____

Love beyond Limits

☺ My Choices

- This week I will choose to recognize God's wonderful, redeeming love for me.

- This week I will choose to walk in his righteous paths.

- This week I will choose to thank him for faithfully wooing me to himself.

- This week I will choose to: _____

_____

_____

_____

_____

_____

 For Further Reading: The Book of Hosea

Plenteous grace with Thee is found,
Grace to cover all my sin;
Let the healing streams abound;
Make and keep me pure within.

CHARLES WESLEY

A Heart of Repentance

 Key Scripture: Joel 2:12–14

That is why the LORD says, "Turn to me now, while there is time! Give me your hearts. Come with fasting, weeping, and mourning. Don't tear your clothing in your grief; instead, tear your hearts." Return to the LORD your God, for he is gracious and merciful. He is not easily angered. He is filled with kindness and is eager not to punish you. Who knows? Perhaps even yet he will give you a reprieve, sending you a blessing instead of this terrible curse. Perhaps he will give you so much that you will be able to offer grain and wine to the LORD your God as before!

The greatest hindrance to revival is pride amongst the Lord's people.

ARTHUR SKEVINGTON WOOD

A Heart of Repentance

 Mom's Reflection

Why this message of repentance? God's people had grown prosperous—and complacent in their relationship with God. Self-centeredness, idolatry, and sin had taken over their hearts. They no longer centered their lives on the Lord; rather, they took him for granted. Joel's message was a stern warning: if the people did not turn from their sinful lifestyle, they would face judgment. Yet within this warning was also a gracious and loving call to repentance.

In many ways Christians today could be described in the same fashion: prosperous, complacent, self-centered, and sinful. Joel's beautiful call to repentance can be an invitation to us as well. We all need to examine our lives, turn from our sin, and draw close to God. Let's replace self-centeredness and complacency with God-centeredness and a fire in our hearts to passionately live for him. May the Lord awake in each of us a true joy and delight in who he is and an eager willingness to obey his Word!

My Thoughts

Are there areas of my life in which God is calling me to repentance? _____

_____

_____

_____

_____

_____

_____

♡ **My Prayer**

"Most loving and gracious Father, I praise you for your mercy. You are patient and kind. I thank you that when I sin, you always invite me to return to your loving embrace. Help me to recognize sin in my life and turn from it. Draw me close to you. Thank you for salvation through your Son, Jesus, who once and for all paid the penalty for my sin. In Jesus's name I pray, amen."

This week I'm praying for:_____

_____

_____

_____

_____

_____

A Heart of Repentance

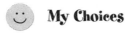 **My Choices**

- This week I will choose to ask the Lord to reveal any sin in my heart from which I need to turn.

- This week I will choose to be less self-centered and more God-centered.

- This week I will choose to reflect on God's grace and mercy toward me.

- This week I will choose to: _____

_____

_____

_____

_____

_____

 For Further Reading: Joel 1–3

You can pray until doomsday for revival, but you will never get it without repentance and confession of sin in the Christian life.

ERLO STEGAN

God's Plumb Line

 Key Scripture: Amos 7:7–9

Then he showed me another vision. I saw the LORD standing beside a wall that had been built using a plumb line. He was checking it with a plumb line to see if it was straight. And the LORD said to me, "Amos, what do you see?"

I answered, "A plumb line."

And the LORD replied, "I will test my people with this plumb line. I will no longer ignore all their sins. The pagan shrines of your ancestors and the temples of Israel will be destroyed, and I will bring the dynasty of King Jeroboam to a sudden end."

A noble book! All men's book! It is our first, oldest statement of the never-ending Problem—man's destiny and God's ways with him here on earth; and all . . . in its sincerity; in its simplicity [and] its epic melody.

THOMAS CARLYLE

God's Plumb Line

 Mom's Reflection

A plumb line is a vital tool for anyone wanting to build a sound and sturdy wall. A simple cord suspending a lead weight, it is used to help a builder determine if the wall he is building is vertically straight. Why does it matter? A crooked wall will eventually collapse. God uses the analogy of the plumb line to represent the measure of sin in our lives. He wants his people to be strong and structurally sound. He knows that sin causes us to go down a crooked path that only leads to our destruction.

What is our plumb line? God's Word. Second Timothy 3:16–17 says, "All Scripture is inspired by God and is useful to teach us what is true and to make us realize what is wrong in our lives. It straightens us out and teaches us to do what is right. It is God's way of preparing us in every way, fully equipped for every good thing God wants us to do."

To build strong lives, we need to measure ourselves against the plumb line of God's Word. To build strong families, we need to use that same plumb line to teach our children how to live lives of obedience to God. Let's send our kids into the world "fully equipped for every good thing" God wants them to do!

 **My Thoughts**

In what ways can I encourage a love for God's Word in my family? _____

_____

_____

_____

_____

_____

_____

My Prayer

"Powerful Lord and gracious Father, I praise you for the wonderful blessing of your Word! Thank you for giving me a plumb line by which I can measure my life. Help me to honor you in the way that I live. Thank you for wanting the best for me and my family. Help us to be "structurally sound" as we study your Word together and learn to walk in your ways. In Jesus's name I pray, amen."

This week I'm praying for:_____

_____

_____

_____

_____

_____

God's Plumb Line

 **My Choices**

- This week I will choose to begin systematically reading God's Word.

- This week I will choose to ask the Lord to reveal any sin that lurks in my heart.

- This week I will choose to teach my children the importance of knowing, loving, and obeying God's Word.

- This week I will choose to: _____

_____

_____

_____

_____

 For Further Reading: Psalm 119

Belief in the Bible, the fruit of deep
meditation, has served me as the guide
of my moral and literary life.
I have found it a capital safely invested,
and richly productive of interest.

JOHANN WOLFGANG VON GOETHE

We Can't Hide from God

 Key Scripture: Jonah 1:1–4

The LORD gave this message to Jonah son of Amittai: "Get up and go to the great city of Nineveh! Announce my judgment against it because I have seen how wicked its people are."

But Jonah got up and went in the opposite direction in order to get away from the LORD. He went down to the seacoast, to the port of Joppa, where he found a ship leaving for Tarshish. He bought a ticket and went on board, hoping that by going away to the west he could escape from the LORD.

But as the ship was sailing along, suddenly the LORD flung a powerful wind over the sea, causing a violent storm that threatened to send them to the bottom.

If any man hopes, in whatever he does, to escape the eye of God, he is grievously wrong.

PINDAR

We Can't Hide from God

 Mom's Reflection

Jonah sounds like a toddler who has just been told to do something he doesn't want to do; he runs the other way. In his little two-year-old mind, he thinks, *I can get away. I can run and hide.* Well, toddlers can run, but they can't hide from Mom! Jonah ran, but he couldn't hide from God.

God's punishment for Jonah was unique and creative: he allowed Jonah to be thrown overboard and swallowed up by a giant fish. In the process God showed Jonah that even in the belly of a giant fish in the deep, vast sea, God was still with him and had a plan for his life. Thankfully, Jonah learned his lesson. When he was eventually deposited on shore, he obeyed God and went straight to Nineveh.

There are many lessons you and I can learn from Jonah's experience, both as God's children and as moms. First and foremost, we can't hide from God. No matter where we go, he will be with us. He can even rescue us from the dark and hopeless situations we create for ourselves. Second, God knows what it's like to have stubborn and disobedient children. He used wise discipline to get Jonah's attention and lead him to obedience. We must do the same with our own kids. Finally, God has a plan and a purpose for our lives. Our best course is always to follow him—not run in the other direction!

My Thoughts

Is there anything in my life right now that I am trying to hide from God?_____

_____

_____

_____

_____

_____

My Prayer

"Great and mighty Father, I praise you for having all power and authority in heaven and on earth. You are able to do all things, and your plans are perfect. Thank you for caring about me and tenderly leading me to follow your ways. Help me to listen to your voice and obey your Word. Grant me wisdom in teaching, training, and disciplining my children, so they learn to be obedient followers of your Word as well. In Jesus's name I pray, amen."

This week I'm praying for:_____

_____

_____

_____

_____

_____

We Can't Hide from God

 My Choices

- This week I will choose to listen to God's direction.

- This week I will choose to share the story of Jonah with my kids.

- This week I will choose to ask the Lord for direction and guidance when it comes to disciplining my children.

- This week I will choose to: _____

_____

_____

_____

_____

For Further Reading: The Book of Jonah

A dying Christian father bade farewell to his family and then turning to his wife said, "My dear, see that you bring the children up to honor and obey you, for if they don't obey you when they are young, they won't obey God when they are older."

HARRY A. IRONSIDE

The Depths of God's Forgiveness

 Key Scripture: Micah 7:18–20

Where is another God like you, who pardons the sins of the survivors among his people? You cannot stay angry with your people forever, because you delight in showing mercy. Once again you will have compassion on us. You will trample our sins under your feet and throw them into the depths of the ocean! You will show us your faithfulness and unfailing love as you promised with an oath to our ancestors Abraham and Jacob long ago.

Among the attributes of God, although they are all equal, mercy shines with even more brilliancy than justice.

MIGUEL DE CERVANTES

The Depths of God's Forgiveness

 Mom's Reflection

The final scene in the Academy Award-winning movie *Titanic* showed the aged heroine, Rose, dropping her treasured diamond necklace into the depths of the ocean— gone forever. It seemed like such an expensive loss; yet to Rose the act was symbolic of being freed from the past.

Our passage in Micah tells us that God throws our sin into the deepest depths of the ocean, freeing us from the weight of past guilt. As believers in Christ we are forgiven completely. God remembers our sin no more.

If God is so willing to forget our sin, shouldn't we do the same? How easy it is for us to hold on to our past sins and mistakes, wallowing in regret! But God wants to free us from the past. He wants to show us unfailing love and compassion so that we might be free "to do what is right, to love mercy, and to walk humbly with [our] God" (Micah 6:8).

What a beautiful way to live!

My Thoughts

Are there any sins from the past that I need to release and forget, knowing God has forgiven me? _____

_____

_____

_____

_____

_____

My Prayer

"Wonderful, loving, and forgiving God, I praise you for your faithfulness and unfailing love. Thank you for forgiving me of all my sins through Jesus. Thank you for throwing those sins into the depths of the ocean. Help me not to fish them out again! I want to live in the freedom you desire for me. Guide me to do what is right, to love mercy, and to walk humbly with you every day of my life. In Jesus's name I pray, amen."

This week I'm praying for:_____

_____

_____

_____

_____

_____

The Depths of God's Forgiveness

 My Choices

- This week I will choose to receive God's mercy and forgiveness through Christ.

- This week I will choose to show mercy toward others.

- This week I will choose to walk humbly with God, knowing that he has pardoned me and loves me with an unfailing love.

- This week I will choose to: _____

_____

_____

_____

_____

For Further Reading: Psalm 103

There's a wideness in God's mercy
Like the wideness of the sea;
There's a kindness in His justice
Which is more than liberty.

FREDERICK WILLIAM FABER

Strength for the Journey

 Key Scripture: Habakkuk 3:18–19

Yet I will rejoice in the LORD! I will be joyful in the God of my salvation. The Sovereign LORD is my strength! He will make me as surefooted as a deer and bring me safely over the mountains.

To have God do his own work through us, even once, is better than a lifetime of human striving.

WATCHMAN NEE

Strength for the Journey

 Mom's Reflection

What are your mountains? Piles of laundry or mail or other to-dos? Responsibilities at home, at work, or in the community? Difficult personal challenges?

Habakkuk's message offers hope to anyone who feels inadequate or overwhelmed: God is sovereign, and he will give us strength. Just as God equips the deer with feet that are able to safely scale the clefts of the mountains, he will equip us with whatever we need to scale the treacherous peaks in our own lives—whether that involves disciplining a difficult child, managing a tough schedule, or simply catching up on the laundry. If we find ourselves in a situation that seems overwhelming, he will provide exactly what we need, step by step, day by day, to make it to the other side.

What a beautiful message for us as moms! We can rejoice—not in our circumstances, but in the Lord. Let's keep our eyes on God, not on the problem in front of us. Then we can say with Habakkuk, "The Sovereign LORD is my strength." He alone will get us safely over every mountain.

My Thoughts

In what areas of my life do I need God's equipping and strength? _____

_____

_____

_____

_____

_____

♡ **My Prayer**

"Wonderful, sovereign Lord, all praise and honor belong to you. I praise you, because you are my strength. I know I can trust you with plans bigger than my own. Thank you for graciously leading me through all the circumstances of my life. Thank you for equipping me with everything I need for my journey. Help me to keep my eyes on you as you lead me safely over every mountain along my way. In Jesus's name I pray, amen."

This week I'm praying for:_____

_____

_____

_____

_____

_____

Strength for the Journey

 My Choices

- This week I will choose to rejoice in the Lord.

- This week I will choose to ask the sovereign Lord for strength.

- This week I will choose to look to God to give me everything I need to make it safely over my mountains.

- This week I will choose to: _____

_____

_____

_____

_____

_____

For Further Reading: Psalms 70; 97

God's might to direct me,
God's power to protect me,
God's wisdom for learning,
God's eye for discerning,
God's ear for my hearing,
God's word for my clearing.

ATTRIBUTED TO ST. PATRICK

His Own Special Treasure

 Key Scripture: Malachi 3:16–18

Then those who feared the LORD spoke with each other, and the LORD listened to what they said. In his presence, a scroll of remembrance was written to record the names of those who feared him and loved to think about him. "They will be my people," says the LORD Almighty. "On the day when I act, they will be my own special treasure. I will spare them as a father spares an obedient and dutiful child. Then you will again see the difference between the righteous and the wicked, between those who serve God and those who do not."

There is a beauty in holiness as well as a beauty of holiness.

GEORGE SWINNOCK

His Own Special Treasure

 Mom's Reflection

"Special treasure." I love that description! If we were to go into an antique store, we would recognize some treasures—items or trinkets that would stand out as precious, valuable, and honored. We'd certainly see some junk as well. Most of the time it's easy to tell the difference. On a rare occasion, though, we may pick up a piece of "junk" and later find out that it was treasure all along.

If we are special treasures of God, then we ought to look like it. Our actions and words ought to be different than the rest of the world's, because we are followers of God. In our passage in Malachi, God confirms that there will be a distinguishable difference between the righteous and the wicked, between those who serve God and those who do not. You and I must ask ourselves, "Is there a distinguishable difference in my life? Does my obedience to Christ show, or do I blend in with the world?"

Always remember that you are a special treasure of God and a beautiful reflection of your Maker. You are not "junk." So let the real you shine through!

Week 31

 ## My Thoughts

In what ways am I like the people described in Malachi 3 who feared God and loved to think and talk about him?

_____

_____

_____

_____

_____

My Prayer

"Wonderful Lord and blessed Creator, I praise you for redeeming my life. Thank you that I am a special treasure to you. Help me to live in a way that honors your love and grace toward me. May the things that I say and do distinguish me as one who follows you all the days of my life. Grant me the wisdom to teach my kids to follow you, and help me to instill in them the truth that they, too, are your special treasures. In Jesus's name I pray, amen."

This week I'm praying for:_____

_____

_____

_____

_____

_____

His Own Special Treasure

☺ My Choices

- This week I will choose to see myself as one of God's treasures.

- This week I will choose to speak and act in ways that reflect I am a follower of God.

- This week I will choose to tell my kids that they are special treasures of God.

- This week I will choose to: _____

_____

_____

_____

_____

_____

 For Further Reading: Psalm 139

The sanctifying grace of God is
appropriated by the obedient
and unrelenting activity
of the regenerate man.

J. A. MOTYER

Why Worry?

 Key Scripture: Matthew 6:31–34

So don't worry about having enough food or drink or clothing. Why be like the pagans who are so deeply concerned about these things? Your heavenly Father already knows all your needs, and he will give you all you need from day to day if you live for him and make the Kingdom of God your primary concern.

So don't worry about tomorrow, for tomorrow will bring its own worries. Today's trouble is enough for today.

Worry does not empty tomorrow of its sorrows; it empties today of its strength.

CORRIE TEN BOOM

Why Worry?

 ## Mom's Reflection

Isn't worrying a mother's right and privilege? We feel almost obligated to worry about the kids' health and homework and friends, not to mention their happiness and self-image and success. There is no shortage of things to worry about as a mom! But Jesus's message in the Sermon on the Mount offers a fresh new perspective. He reminds us that our heavenly Father knows our needs (much better than we do, by the way), and he will give us what we need from day to day.

As we seek God's kingdom first and make it our central focus, all of these other things will fall into proper perspective. Jesus is not downplaying the importance of caring for our kids, being responsible, and doing what needs to be done; but he is imploring us not to be consumed with worry, which keeps us from pursuing what really matters in life. As moms let's choose to live one day at a time. Let's relinquish worry and fill our hearts and minds with God first. We'll be better off for it—and so will our children.

My Thoughts

What do I tend to worry about? Am I willing to give those areas of concern over to God? _____

_____

_____

_____

_____

_____

♡ My Prayer

"Wonderful and glorious Lord, I praise you, because you are the one who meets my needs. I praise you for your care for me and my family. Thank you that you don't want me to worry but rather to turn my thoughts toward you. Help me, Father, to keep my focus on things that really matter. Help me to relinquish worry and fretting and to make your kingdom my primary concern. In Jesus's name I pray, amen."

This week I'm praying for:_____

_____

_____

_____

_____

_____

Why Worry?

 My Choices

- This week I will choose to focus my heart and mind on God's kingdom.

- This week I will choose to worry less and pray more.

- This week I will choose to live responsibly today and not fret about tomorrow.

- This week I will choose to: _____

_____

_____

_____

_____

_____

 For Further Reading: Matthew 5–7

Worry is like a rocking chair.
It gives you something to do but
doesn't get you anywhere.

AUTHOR UNKNOWN

The Beauty of Service

 Key Scripture: Mark 10:42–45

So Jesus called them together and said, "You know that in this world kings are tyrants, and officials lord it over the people beneath them. But among you it should be quite different. Whoever wants to be a leader among you must be your servant, and whoever wants to be first must be the slave of all. For even I, the Son of Man, came here not to be served but to serve others, and to give my life as a ransom for many."

There are no trivial assignments in the work of the Lord.

VANCE HAVNER

The Beauty of Service

 Mom's Reflection

Certainly mothers know what it's like to serve. A mom's job never seems to end. Her responsibilities range from caring for the kids to dealing with the laundry to driving in the carpool, and everything in between. In the world's eyes, motherhood may not seem like a glorious profession; but in God's eyes it is highly honorable. Jesus himself said the ones who are greatest in God's kingdom are those who are servants of all.

When we grow tired and weary in our service to our families, we can ask God for strength to do what he calls us to do. After all, he has already gone before us, giving us an example of servant leadership. It's easy to want to claim our rights. "I deserve _____." "I have a right to _____." "It's not fair that I have to _____." But Jesus didn't claim his right to the glory and honor due him when he walked this earth. He simply served. He willingly laid his life down for us. Aren't you glad we have such a wonderful Lord?

Week 33

💡 My Thoughts

In what ways do I find joy in serving my family? _____

_____

_____

_____

_____

_____

_____

♡ My Prayer

"Great and glorious Lord, I praise you for the wonder of your Son, Jesus, who offered his life as a sacrifice for me. I'm thankful that you value a servant's heart. Give me the strength to keep serving, even when I grow tired and weary. Help me to keep your example foremost in my mind. Thank you for always being with me. In Jesus's name I pray, amen."

This week I'm praying for: _____

_____

_____

_____

_____

_____

_____

The Beauty of Service

😊 **My Choices**

- This week I will choose to serve my family with joy.
- This week I will choose to see my role of service to others as something of value in God's kingdom.
- This week I will choose to thank the Lord for the example he set of servant leadership.
- This week I will choose to: _____

_____

_____

_____

_____

_____

 For Further Reading: Philippians 2

The world's idea of greatness
is to rule, but Christian greatness
consists in serving.

J. C. RYLE

One Baby, One Night

 Key Scripture: Luke 2:8–14

That night some shepherds were in the fields outside the village, guarding their flocks of sheep. Suddenly, an angel of the Lord appeared among them, and the radiance of the Lord's glory surrounded them. They were terribly frightened, but the angel reassured them. "Don't be afraid!" he said. "I bring you good news of great joy for everyone! The Savior—yes, the Messiah, the Lord—has been born tonight in Bethlehem, the city of David! And this is how you will recognize him: You will find a baby lying in a manger, wrapped snugly in strips of cloth!"

Suddenly, the angel was joined by a vast host of others—the armies of heaven—praising God:

"Glory to God in the highest heaven,
and peace on earth to all whom God favors."

One Baby, One Night

 Mom's Reflection

Not only were the shepherds scared, but they must have been bewildered. They found the savior of the whole world, the long-awaited Messiah, lying in a *feeding trough*? But God's ways are perfect. No doubt those shepherds (not to mention you and I) would have chosen a safe and sanitary royal crib for the King of kings. But God chose the approachable rather than the affluent for his Son's first surroundings.

Isn't it amazing? This one baby born on this one night would forever change all of history! As the angel declared, "The Savior—yes, the Messiah, the Lord—has been born," and he brings peace "to all whom God favors." By "peace," the angel wasn't talking about peace between men, but rather peace with God. No longer would mankind have to offer sacrifices for his sin; the Savior, Jesus, had come into the world, and one day he would lay down his life as the final, perfect sacrifice, providing peace with God for all who believe.

On that first night, though, he was laid in a simple manger—not in a royal nursery surrounded by servants and guards. He was approachable back then to simple shepherds. He is approachable today to you and me. No matter what our lives are like, we can come to him and say, "I believe you are the Son of God. I believe you died for me. I trust you as my savior." And from that moment forward, we can have peace with God.

My Thoughts

What does Jesus mean to me personally? Is he simply someone whose birthday I celebrate at Christmas, or is he much more? _____

_____

_____

_____

_____

My Prayer

"Wonderful Lord, I praise you for sending your Son, Jesus, to be born as a humble baby. Thank you for his life here on earth. Thank you for the words he spoke. Thank you for the compassion he showed. Most importantly, thank you that he died and rose again. What amazing love! Help me to understand the significance of his birth to me personally, and help me to share that significance with my children. May they, too, come to know him as their personal Lord and Savior. In Jesus's name I pray, amen."

This week I'm praying for:_____

_____

_____

_____

_____

One Baby, One Night

😊 My Choices

- This week I will choose to praise the Lord for the gift of his Son, Jesus.

- This week I will choose to reflect on what Christ's birth means to me.

- This week I will choose to share the wonder of his birth with my children.

- This week I will choose to: _____

_____

_____

_____

_____

_____

 For Further Reading: Luke 1–2

> When God spoke to humanity
> in Jesus, he said the last thing
> he has to say.
>
> G. Campbell Morgan

The Ultimate Travel Information

 Key Scripture: John 14:1–6

"Don't be troubled. You trust God, now trust in me. There are many rooms in my Father's home, and I am going to prepare a place for you. If this were not so, I would tell you plainly. When everything is ready, I will come and get you, so that you will always be with me where I am. And you know where I am going and how to get there."

"No, we don't know, Lord," Thomas said. "We haven't any idea where you are going, so how can we know the way?"

Jesus told him, "I am the way, the truth, and the life. No one can come to the Father except through me."

Salvation is a happy security and a secure happiness.

William Jenkyn

The Ultimate Travel Information

 ## Mom's Reflection

Have you ever started out on a trip without good directions or a reliable map? It's scary! Personally, I always try to get the best travel information I can before leaving home. Having that map in hand gives me a great sense of comfort and security.

In this passage in John, Jesus didn't want his followers to be troubled about the future, so he began telling them that he would soon be going away to prepare a place for them in his Father's house. He wanted them to know where they would be going and how they would get there. He was providing them with the ultimate travel information!

The disciples were still a little unclear, however, so they inquired further. I'm so glad they did, because Jesus couldn't have been clearer in his response: "I am the way, the truth and the life. No one can come to the Father except through me."

All of us are on a journey called life. Thankfully, God has provided us with all the travel information we need. Destination: heaven. Path to get there: Jesus. Some may say, "That road is too narrow." But in reality it's wide enough for all who accept it. Jesus is our way to the Father. He is the embodiment and fulfillment of God's truth, and he provides life for us both now and for eternity. What greater comfort or security could there be?

💡 My Thoughts

Do I see Jesus as the way, the truth, and the life in my life?

_____

_____

_____

_____

_____

_____

🗘 My Prayer

"Loving Father, I praise you for having a plan for my life. It is a wonderful plan. Thank you for paying the price for my entrance to heaven by sending your Son, Jesus. He is the way, the truth, and the life. Thank you for making my travel directions so clear! Help me to direct others down that same clear path. In Jesus's name I pray, amen."

This week I'm praying for:_____

_____

_____

_____

_____

_____

_____

The Ultimate Travel Information

☺ My Choices

- This week I will choose to trust Christ as the way to the Father.

- This week I will choose to recognize him as the fulfillment of God's truth and the source of my life, both now and forever.

- This week I will choose to share this great "travel information" with others.

- This week I will choose to: _____

_____

_____

_____

 For Further Reading: John 14–15

> That Christ and a forgiven sinner
> should be made one, and share heaven
> between them, is the wonder of
> salvation; what more could love do?
>
> SAMUEL RUTHERFORD

We Are Not Alone

 Key Scripture: Acts 1:6–11

When the apostles were with Jesus, they kept asking him, "Lord, are you going to free Israel now and restore our kingdom?"

"The Father sets those dates," he replied, "and they are not for you to know. But when the Holy Spirit has come upon you, you will receive power and will tell people about me everywhere—in Jerusalem, throughout Judea, in Samaria, and to the ends of the earth."

It was not long after he said this that he was taken up into the sky while they were watching, and he disappeared into a cloud. As they were straining their eyes to see him, two white-robed men suddenly stood there among them. They said, "Men of Galilee, why are you standing here staring at the sky? Jesus has been taken away from you into heaven. And someday, just as you saw him go, he will return!"

We Are Not Alone

 Mom's Reflection

"Don't go! Oh please don't go!" I'm sure the disciples were thinking it, if not saying it. What would they do without their leader, their friend, their guide? But in God's plan it was time for Jesus to leave the earth. By his life and with his death, he would accomplish everything God had sent him to do. He was not going to leave the disciples alone, however. In his grace God was going to send his Holy Spirit to give them power and strength to carry on Jesus's message.

How incredible to think that God would send his Spirit to live inside his disciples—and inside us! Once the Holy Spirit came, the disciples would no longer need to feel afraid, lonely, or confused. We no longer need to feel afraid, lonely, or confused either. As Christ's followers we, too, have received his Spirit, who lives and dwells within us. We are never alone. What a wonderful assurance! As we tend to our children, we are not alone. As we do our laundry, he is with us. When we shop for groceries, he is right there. Let's recognize and enjoy his presence in our lives.

My Thoughts

Am I aware of God's constant presence with me? How do I experience his presence in my life?_____

_____

_____

_____

_____

_____

My Prayer

"Glorious Lord, High King of Heaven, I praise you for your power and majesty! I stand amazed that the God of all creation would want to dwell in my life. Thank you for your Holy Spirit, who leads me, teaches me, and comforts me. Help me to find joy each day in your presence. Lead me and guide me as I take care of my body, knowing that it is the place where your Spirit dwells. In Jesus's name I pray, amen."

This week I'm praying for:_____

_____

_____

_____

_____

_____

We Are Not Alone

😊 My Choices

- This week I will choose to thank the Lord for giving me his Spirit to dwell in me.

- This week I will choose to reflect on the Holy Spirit's presence in my life.

- This week I will choose to enjoy the fact that God's Spirit is with me, and I am never alone.

- This week I will choose to: _____

_____

_____

_____

_____

_____

 For Further Reading: John 16; Acts 1–2

Come, Holy Spirit, God and Lord!
Be all thy graces now outpoured
On the believer's mind and heart,
Your fervent love to us impart.

MARTIN LUTHER

Nothing Can Separate Us

 Key Scripture: Romans 8:35–39

Can anything ever separate us from Christ's love? Does it mean he no longer loves us if we have trouble or calamity, or are persecuted, or are hungry or cold or in danger or threatened with death? (Even the Scriptures say, "For your sake we are killed every day; we are being slaughtered like sheep.") No, despite all these things, overwhelming victory is ours through Christ, who loved us.

And I am convinced that nothing can ever separate us from his love. Death can't, and life can't. The angels can't, and the demons can't. Our fears for today, our worries about tomorrow, and even the powers of hell can't keep God's love away. Whether we are high above the sky or in the deepest ocean, nothing in all creation will ever be able to separate us from the love of God that is revealed in Christ Jesus our Lord.

Nothing Can Separate Us

 Mom's Reflection

Can you imagine your children ever doing something so disobedient, so wrong that you would stop loving them altogether? OK, you may not like them every minute of the day, but you love them completely. They could never step out of the bounds of your love. If we, being mere mortals, have such an abiding love for our children, how much more does our great and perfect heavenly Father love us?

The scripture is clear: We cannot step out of his love. Nothing can separate us from his love. We can't go anywhere on this earth to get away from his love. What great comfort and joy there is to know that we are completely, passionately loved by him! Earthly love is limited; but his love has no limits, no boundaries, no stopping point. Relish this fact! Reflect on it when your life is running smoothly. Hold on to it when your world seems to be falling apart, or when you've made a big mistake. Know that he loves you—and his love will never change.

My Thoughts

How does it help me in my daily life to know that nothing can separate me from God's love? _____

_____

_____

_____

_____

_____

_____

♡ My Prayer

"Perfect Father, Lover of my soul, I praise you for your limitless love! I praise you that your love is sure and true, proven by the gift of your Son, Jesus. Thank you that I am a recipient of your love. I value you it. I relish it. I need it. Thank you that I am forever secure in your perfect love. Help me to reflect your love to my children and to all the people around me. In Jesus's name I pray, amen."

This week I'm praying for:_____

_____

_____

_____

_____

_____

Nothing Can Separate Us

 My Choices

- This week I will choose to appreciate and relish God's great love for me.

- This week I will choose to reflect his love to those around me.

- This week I will choose to teach my children that nothing can separate us from the love of Christ.

- This week I will choose to: _____

_____

_____

_____

_____

For Further Reading: Romans 5; 8; 12

Before you were conceived, I wanted you.
Before you were born, I loved you.
Before you were here
an hour, I would die for you.
This is the miracle of life.

MAUREEN HAWKINS

Troubles to Triumph

 Key Scripture: 2 Corinthians
34:16–18

*That is why we never give up. Though our bodies
are dying, our spirits are being renewed every
day. For our present troubles are quite small and
won't last very long. Yet they produce for us an
immeasurably great glory that will last forever! So
we don't look at the troubles we can see right now;
rather, we look forward to what we have not yet
seen. For the troubles we see will soon be over, but
the joys to come will last forever.*

Troubles are often the tools by which
God fashions us for better things.

HENRY WARD BEECHER

Troubles to Triumph

 Mom's Reflection

"Are we there yet?" "How much longer till we get there?"

Every road trip has its ups and downs, twists and turns; but the joy comes when we reach our destination. In this passage in 2 Corinthians, we read Paul's encouragement to the early Christians to keep their eyes on their wonderful destination, not on the momentary troubles of their journey. It's a message for us as well. God wants us to understand that the road trip here on earth may have some twists and bumps along the way, but the challenges we face will ultimately produce an immeasurably great eternal glory.

In our homes we must keep the big picture in mind. It's easy to let the little things of daily life agitate us and get us down. We need Paul's reminder to take our eyes off our light, momentary troubles and place our focus on what is really important and lasting. Instead of focusing on our pain, discomfort, or challenges, let's change our focus to look with hope at what God can and will do in our lives. Don't give up and don't lose heart! As Paul says, our spirits are being renewed each day.

Just as our kids must trust us as we drive them to their destination, we must trust our heavenly Father, knowing that he has a perfect plan for our lives. Let's replace our grumbling with anticipation, our whining with hope. Our positive attitude will make for a much more delightful ride!

Week 38

 My Thoughts

How do I need to change my focus concerning the challenges I face? _____

_____

_____

_____

_____

_____

My Prayer

"Wonderful Lord, I praise you for having a perfect plan for my life. Thank you for being with me each step of this journey. Help me to keep my eyes off momentary troubles and discomforts and, instead, keep my eyes on you and the eternal glory that awaits me in your presence. Renew my spirit day by day. Help me to never give up but rather to persevere with hope. In Jesus's name I pray, amen."

This week I'm praying for:_____

_____

_____

_____

_____

_____

Troubles to Triumph

 **My Choices**

- This week I will choose to take my eyes off my troubles.

- This week I will choose to focus on the bigger, eternal picture.

- This week I will choose to place my hope in the Lord and trust his plan for my life.

- This week I will choose to: _____

_____

_____

_____

_____

 For Further Reading: 2 Corinthians 4–5

When the outlook is dark,
And the in-look's discouraging,
Just try the up-look;
It's always encouraging.

AUTHOR UNKNOWN

Love That Builds Up

 Key Scripture: Galatians 5:13–15

*For you, dear friends, have been called to live
in freedom—not freedom to satisfy your sinful
nature, but freedom to serve one another in love.
For the whole law can be summed up in this one
command: "Love your neighbor as yourself." But
if instead of showing love among yourselves you are
always biting and devouring one another, watch
out! Beware of destroying one another.*

Go home and love your family.

MOTHER TERESA, when asked, "What can we
do to promote world peace?"

Love That Builds Up

 **Mom's Reflection**

Recently, on a chalkboard in my kitchen, I wrote the words, "Top Priorities." Underneath the heading I wrote:

"Number One: Love God.

Number Two: Love others."

These are the two biggies. They cover it all! Wouldn't the world be a different place if we actually lived as though they were our top priorities?

In this passage Paul warns us against destroying one another with our words or actions. How easy it is for one family member to tear down another with unkind words and a nit-picking, critical eye! But that's not loving God or loving others. Love sees the good in others and encourages the best in others. Love overlooks faults and yet lovingly disciplines.

Let's make sure that love reigns in our homes, beginning with us as moms. Let's set the example and determine to see the good in our spouses and children. After all, God calls us not to devour one another, but rather to build one another up in love.

My Thoughts

How am I showing God's love in practical ways in my home?

_____

_____

_____

_____

_____

_____

My Prayer

"Loving Lord, I praise you for being the perfect picture of love. Thank you for showing me what love looks like by sending your Son, Jesus, to die for me. Oh Lord, help me to serve my family in love! Guard my heart from being critical, and keep me from devouring others with my words or actions. Help me to genuinely love my family and all the other people you place in my life. In Jesus's name I pray, amen."

This week I'm praying for:_____

_____

_____

_____

_____

_____

Love That Builds Up

:-) My Choices

- This week I will choose to see the best in my husband and children.

- This week I will choose to guard my heart and mind from being critical of others.

- This week I will choose to teach my children the importance of serving one another in love.

- This week I will choose to: _____

_____

_____

_____

_____

For Further Reading: 1 Corinthians 13; Galatians 5

> If God should have no more mercy on us than we have charity one to another, what would become of us?
>
> THOMAS FULLER

Victory over Anger

 Key Scripture: Ephesians 4:21–27

Since you have heard all about him and have learned the truth that is in Jesus, throw off your old evil nature and your former way of life, which is rotten through and through, full of lust and deception. Instead, there must be a spiritual renewal of your thoughts and attitudes. You must display a new nature because you are a new person, created in God's likeness—righteous, holy, and true.

So put away all falsehood and "tell your neighbor the truth" because we belong to each other. And "don't sin by letting anger gain control over you." Don't let the sun go down while you are still angry, for anger gives a mighty foothold to the Devil.

Anger is momentary madness, so control your passion or it will control you.

HORACE

Victory over Anger

 Mom's Reflection

Anger. Maybe it was never a big problem for you until you had kids. But somehow, as your children's lives progressed through diapers and tantrums to teenage hormones, anger has become a common emotion that erupts from you, seemingly out of nowhere. Let me assure you, you are not alone. Most moms feel frustrated and angry at times. Anger is a normal emotion. It's what we do with it that matters.

In Ephesians Paul encourages us to not allow anger to gain control over us. If we vent our anger with screams or thoughtless rage, we hurt others and rarely accomplish anything good. If we keep our anger bottled up inside us, it can grow into bitterness and resentment. If we nurse our anger and hold on to our hurts, we give the devil an opportunity to destroy relationships within our families and our communities.

We need to deal with our anger in an appropriate way— a way that builds up and doesn't tear down. Instead of responding to your kids (or anyone else) in anger, take a few minutes to calm down; take several deep breaths; and try to see the other person's perspective. Pray for God's wisdom and self-control, then deal with the issue in a calm strength. Do it before the day is through!

Week 40

💡 My Thoughts

Do I have any areas of uncontrolled anger that I need to give over to the Lord? _____

_____

_____

_____

_____

_____

♡ My Prayer

"Great and mighty Lord, I praise you for your power, which can calm a raging sea. Thank you for the way you calm my spirit and give me self-control. Day by day I need your wisdom and direction, Lord; moment by moment I need your strength. Help me to handle my anger in the right way, especially in my family. Please don't let anger, bitterness, or rage take over my heart. Fill my heart with love and forgiveness instead. In Jesus's name I pray, amen."

This week I'm praying for:_____

_____

_____

_____

_____

_____

Victory over Anger

 **My Choices**

- This week I will choose to deal with my anger in the proper way.

- This week I will choose to ask the Lord for wisdom and self-control.

- This week I will choose to not let the sun go down on my anger.

- This week I will choose to: _____

_____

_____

_____

_____

 For Further Reading: Ephesians 4–5

If you would learn self-mastery,
begin by yielding yourself
to the One Great Master.

JOHANN FRIEDRICH LOBSTEIN

Experiencing Joy and Peace

 Key Scripture: Philippians 4:4–9

Always be full of joy in the Lord. I say it again—rejoice! Let everyone see that you are considerate in all you do. Remember, the Lord is coming soon.

Don't worry about anything; instead, pray about everything. Tell God what you need, and thank him for all he has done. If you do this, you will experience Gods' peace, which is far more wonderful than the human mind can understand. His peace will guard your hearts and minds as you live in Christ Jesus.

And now dear brothers and sisters, let me say one more thing as I close this letter. Fix your thoughts on what is true and honorable and right. Think about things that are pure and lovely and admirable. Think about things that are excellent and worthy of praise. Keep putting into practice all you learned from me and heard from me and saw me doing, and the God of peace will be with you.

Experiencing Joy and Peace

 Mom's Reflection

Joy and peace. What beautiful attributes! What mom wouldn't want to have more joy and peace in her life? Thankfully, God has given us principles that can make joy and peace greater realities for each of us—even in the midst of day-to-day family chaos.

First, we need to choose to be joyful. As Christians we have reason to rejoice, but so often we get bogged down with the cares and worries of daily life. Choose joy! Second, we need to replace worry with prayer and thanksgiving. As we pray about our concerns and thank the Lord for what he is doing in our lives, our perspective changes and God gives us a peace "which is far more wonderful than the human mind can understand." Third, we need to focus on what is good in our lives, not on what is wrong. We must be diligent to change our pattern of thinking!

If we put these principles into practice, Paul says, then the God of peace will be with us. I want that for you and for me. I want God's peace and joy to permeate our homes, changing not only our own lives but our children's lives too.

My Thoughts

Do joy and peace permeate my life and home? How can I experience more of both?_____

_____

_____

_____

_____

_____

♡ My Prayer

"God of peace, I praise you and thank you for the peace I have with you because of Jesus's death on the cross. Thank you for the peace you give me in my heart. Thank you for the peace you enable me to experience with others through your love. Help me to be a mom who is filled with joy and peace, and help my kids to learn to experience your joy and peace as they grow to know you better. Help me to be a blessed example for them. In Jesus's name I pray, amen."

This week I'm praying for:_____

_____

_____

_____

_____

_____

Experiencing Joy and Peace

☺ My Choices

- This week I will choose to rejoice in the Lord.

- This week I will choose to pray instead of worry.

- This week I will choose to thank the Lord for all he is doing in my life and my home.

- This week I will choose to: _____

_____

_____

_____

_____

_____

 For Further Reading: The Book of Philippians

The word *joy* is too great and grand
to be confused with the superficial
things we call happiness.
It was joy and peace which Jesus . . .
left us in his will.

KIRBY PAGE

A View of Eternity

 Key Scripture: Colossians 3:1–4

Since you have been raised to new life with Christ, set your sights on the realities of heaven, where Christ sits at God's right hand in the place of honor and power. Let heaven fill your thoughts. Do not think only about things down here on earth. For you died when Christ died, and your real life is hidden with Christ in God. And when Christ, who is your real life, is revealed to the whole world, you will share in all his glory.

He who has no vision of eternity will never get a true hold of time.

THOMAS CARLYLE

A View of Eternity

 Mom's Reflection

How do we keep our eyes on the realities of heaven when the realities at home include hungry kids, dirty floors, and running late to soccer practice? Challenges, crises, and the simple, daily routines of life can blur our vision, allowing us to see only what is right in front of our eyes. But Paul exhorts us to step back and look at the bigger picture. An eternal perspective reminds us that God is with us, and he has a plan and a purpose for us. Eternity-focused eyes give us a clearer, healthier perspective on temporary things.

After all, our real lives are hidden with Christ in God. We are safe and secure in him. And one day we will be with Him in glory! Let's keep sight of the fact that Christ is ready and willing to help us through the crises, teach us through the challenges, and strengthen us through the chores of daily life. He is seated at God's right hand, and he has the power to help us live each day with eternity in mind.

Week 42

My Thoughts

Do I keep my main focus on my circumstances or on the Lord?_____

_____

_____

_____

_____

_____

My Prayer

"God of glory, I praise you, for you are the maker of heaven and earth. I praise you, for you are above all things, and by you all things exist. I confess that my eyes are easily focused on the daily activities and immediate needs that are right in front of me. Help me to see the bigger picture, knowing that you have an eternal plan. Allow me to remember that you are with me and your power and strength are real in my life. In Jesus's name I pray, amen."

This week I'm praying for:_____

_____

_____

_____

_____

_____

A View of Eternity

 **My Choices**

- This week I will choose to see God at work in my life and in the lives of those around me.

- This week I will choose to value eternal things more than material and temporal things.

- This week I will choose to see my children as eternal souls who are "works in progress."

- This week I will choose to: _____

_____

_____

_____

_____

 For Further Reading: The Book of Colossians

> If we look around us, a moment can seem a long time, but when we lift up our hearts heavenwards, a thousand years begin to be like a moment.
>
> JOHN CALVIN

Positive Principles for Life

 Key Scripture: 1 Thessalonians 5:14–18

Brothers and sisters, we urge you to warn those who are lazy. Encourage those who are timid. Take tender care of those who are weak. Be patient with everyone.

See that no one pays back evil for evil, but always try to do good to each other and to everyone else.

Always be joyful. Keep on praying. No matter what happens, always be thankful, for this is God's will for you who belong to Christ Jesus.

Gratitude to God makes even a temporal blessing a taste of heaven.

WILLIAM ROMAINE

Positive Principles for Life

 Mom's Reflection

Short, sweet, and to the point! I like Paul's style. In a few brief verses, he packs a powerful punch. Here we read several positive principles for getting along with others and getting along in life: warn the lazy, encourage the timid, tenderly care for the weak, be patient with everyone. Is it just me, or does Paul sound like he could be talking specifically to moms? We would do well to apply these four principles to our daily parenting skills!

His next statement can be applied to family interactions, too, especially between siblings: don't pay back evil for evil, but do good to each other. Perhaps we should have our kids memorize that one!

Finally, Paul gives us the "how-to" part. The first principle we have heard before: "Always be joyful." In other words, choose to rejoice. The second principle is closely related: "Keep on praying." Joy comes naturally when we keep our hearts continually pointed heavenward through prayer and when we thank the Lord in all circumstances. As moms we can experience God's joy and love for the people around us by keeping a prayerful and thankful attitude throughout each day.

Week 43

My Thoughts

Am I encouraging and caring for my family with joy and
thankfulness?_____

_____

_____

_____

_____

_____

My Prayer

"God of grace and peace, I praise you for the joy and
strength only you can give. Thank you for the people in
my life. Help me to tenderly care for them and patiently
encourage them. Thank you for the way you are working
through the circumstances of my life right now. I may not
like every circumstance, but I know you are with me. Help
me to be joyful, thankful, and prayerful. Thank you for your
faithfulness in all things. In Jesus's name I pray, amen."

This week I'm praying for:_____

_____

_____

_____

_____

_____

Positive Principles for Life

 **My Choices**

- This week I will choose to tenderly care for and encourage those around me.

- This week I will choose to remain prayerful throughout each day.

- This week I will choose to thank the Lord continually and encourage my children to do the same.

- This week I will choose to: _____

_____

_____

_____

_____

 For Further Reading: The Book of 1 Thessalonians

> God is pleased with no music below
> so much as with the thanksgiving
> songs . . . of rejoicing, comforted
> and thankful persons.
>
> JEREMY TAYLOR

Family Resemblance

 Key Scripture: 2 Timothy 1:5–8

I know that you sincerely trust the Lord, for you have the faith of your mother, Eunice, and your grandmother, Lois. This is why I remind you to fan into flames the spiritual gift God gave you when I laid my hands on you. For God has not given us a spirit of fear and timidity, but of power, love, and self-discipline. So you must never be ashamed to tell others about our Lord.

Every believer is a witness whether he wants to be or not.

DONALD GREY BARNHOUSE

Family Resemblance

 Mom's Reflection

What a beautiful family portrait! Timothy came from a heritage of faith. Both his mother and grandmother had a strong and abiding walk with the Lord. Now Paul could see that same strong faith in Timothy.

As moms we want our kids (and grandkids) to develop an active and vibrant faith in the Lord. How does that happen? It begins with our example. It continues with our words. Paul told Timothy not to be shy or ashamed to tell others about the Lord. We need to heed that counsel when it comes to sharing our faith with our kids. After all, "God has not given us a spirit of fear and timidity, but of power, love, and self-discipline." May that spirit be evident in our lives as we share our faith in Jesus with our children!

Often when my daughter and I are together, people say, "Oh, she looks just like you." It is my eternal hope that my faith example would be so strong, people would see my faith reflected in hers as well. There is no greater family resemblance than that of a strong faith passed on from generation to generation.

Week 44

💡 My Thoughts

How do I currently share my faith with my family?

_____

_____

_____

_____

_____

♡ My Prayer

"Gracious and powerful Lord, I praise you for your Spirit of power, love, and self-discipline. I thank you for the Holy Spirit's work in my life. Please give me power to share my faith. Grant me love to show my faith. Allow me to have self-discipline to live out my faith in obedience to you. Please help me, by my words and my example, to pass on a strong faith to my children. In Jesus's name I pray, amen."

This week I'm praying for:_____

_____

_____

_____

_____

_____

Family Resemblance

 My Choices

- This week I will choose to ask the Lord to make his power, love, and self-discipline evident in my life.

- This week I will choose to share my faith with my family through my words and actions.

- This week I will choose to use the spiritual gifts God has given me.

- This week I will choose to: _____

_____

_____

_____

_____

For Further Reading: The Book of 2 Timothy

> Love—and the unity it attests to—is the mark Christ gave Christians to wear before the world. Only with this mark may the world know that Christians are indeed Christians and that Jesus was sent by the Father.
>
> FRANCIS SCHAEFFER

Woman to Woman

 Key Scripture: Titus 2:3–5

Similarly, teach the older women to live in a way that is appropriate for someone serving the Lord. They must not go around speaking evil of others and must not be heavy drinkers. Instead, they should teach others what is good. These older women must train the younger women to love their husbands and their children, to live wisely and be pure, to take care of their homes, to do good, and to be submissive to their husbands. Then they will not bring shame on the word of God.

Earth has nothing more tender than a woman's heart when it is the abode of piety.

MARTIN LUTHER

Woman to Woman

 ## Mom's Reflection

Women need each other—to encourage each other, offer support, and strengthen one another. Just as iron sharpens iron, so God can use one woman to sharpen another, making both women stronger, wiser, and more useful in God's kingdom.

In this passage in Titus, we see the older women being encouraged to train up the younger women. In today's lingo we call this mentoring. No matter what stage of life you're in, you can be involved in mentoring. If you're older, maybe it's time to share your knowledge and experience by reaching out to a younger mom; if you're younger, perhaps you'd benefit from the help and encouragement of an older woman who has already gone through what you're experiencing.

Ask the Lord to lead you to someone who can join you in a mentoring relationship. As women let's commit to strengthening one another in the work the Lord has given us to do.

💡 My Thoughts

Is there a mentoring relationship I need to develop? _____

_____

_____

_____

_____

_____

_____

🤍 My Prayer

"Great and mighty Lord, I praise you for your love and kindness toward me. Thank you for the blessing of my family. Thank you, too, for the women you have brought into my life to help me, encourage me, support me, and strengthen me. Help me to be a strong, reliable support to other women as well. Lead me to the right mentoring relationships in every stage of my life. May your love shine through me in all that I do. In Jesus's name I pray, amen."

This week I'm praying for:_____

_____

_____

_____

_____

_____

Woman to Woman

 My Choices

- This week I will choose to connect with another woman for encouragement and support.

- This week I will choose to be an encouragement to a friend.

- This week I will choose to be a godly example for other women to follow.

- This week I will choose to: _____

_____

_____

_____

_____

For Further Reading: The Book of Titus

A beautiful and chaste woman is
the perfect workmanship of God,
and the true glory of the angels,
the rare miracle of earth, and
the sole wonder of the world.

GEORG HERMES

The Joy of Generosity

 Key Scripture: Philemon 4–7

I always thank God when I pray for you, Philemon, because I keep hearing of your trust in the Lord Jesus and your love for all of God's people. You are generous because of your faith. And I am praying that you will really put your generosity to work, for in so doing you will come to an understanding of all the good things we can do for Christ. I myself have gained much joy and comfort from your love, my brother, because your kindness has so often refreshed the hearts of God's people.

A giving Savior should have giving disciples.

J. C. RYLE

The Joy of Generosity

 ## Mom's Reflection

Often we think of generosity in terms of financial or material donations. Certainly, donations can fall under the label of "generosity"; but to be honest, many times "obligation," "pride," or "tax relief" would be more accurate descriptions. According to God's Word, generosity is a lifestyle born out of our faith in God and love for others. There are many ways we can live generous lives. Consider generosity in the areas of kindness or forgiveness. How different would our world be if we were all generous in those areas? And what about being generous with our time and talents?

Think for a moment about what you can give generously to others. It may be a listening ear, words of encouragement, or help with the kids. Perhaps you can cook a meal or give a piano lesson or teach a class. Whatever you do, I guarantee you'll be blessed. There's no greater joy than the joy of giving generously of ourselves to others. If you're feeling down or blue, practice generosity by blessing someone else—then watch how fast your blues dissipate!

Week 46

💡 **My Thoughts**

In what ways do I show generosity to others? _____

_____

_____

_____

_____

_____

💛 **My Prayer**

"Loving and giving heavenly Father, I praise you for your generosity toward me. Thank you for not even withholding your only Son but giving him as a sacrifice for my sins. Thank you for giving me your Holy Spirit, and thank you for the gifts he brings to my life. You are the ultimate picture of generosity born of love! Help me to love others with a pure and generous love, beginning with my family and overflowing to others around me. Show me what and how I can give. In Jesus's name I pray, amen."

This week I'm praying for:_____

_____

_____

_____

_____

_____

The Joy of Generosity

 My Choices

- This week I will choose to consider ways I can give generously to others.

- This week I will choose to reach out to someone and share what I can give.

- This week I will choose to be generous in kindness and forgiveness.

- This week I will choose to: _____

_____

_____

_____

_____

_____

For Further Reading: Luke 6

We give Thee but Thine own,
Whate'er the gift may be:
All that we have is Thine alone,
A trust, O Lord, from Thee.

WILLIAM W. HOW

A Gracious Invitation

 Key Scripture: Hebrews 4:14–16

That is why we have a great High Priest who has gone to heaven, Jesus the Son of God. Let us cling to him and never stop trusting him. This High Priest of ours understands our weaknesses, for he faced all of the same temptations we do, yet he did not sin. So let us come boldly to the throne of our gracious God. There we will receive his mercy, and we will find grace to help us when we need it.

Because God is the living God, He can hear; because He is a loving God, He will hear; because He is our covenant God, He has bound Himself to hear.

CHARLES H. SPURGEON

A Gracious Invitation

 ## Mom's Reflection

If a son needs help with his homework, he goes to Mom. If a daughter falls and scrapes her knee, she runs to Mom. When Dad can't find a matching pair of socks, he yells for Mom. Mom is definitely the go-to person when it comes to keeping the home running smoothly. But who does Mom go to when she needs help?

Our passage this week is a wonderful reminder that we have a gracious heavenly Father who beckons us to come to him. No need is too small. No sin is too big. We can come boldly before God's throne because we have a High Priest, Jesus, who not only understands us, he gave his life for us. Because of his sacrifice on our behalf, we are clean and new and forgiven before God.

Now Christ sits at the right hand of God as our advocate. What do we find when we come to him? Mercy and grace to help us when we need it! Dear friend, let's commit to starting each day at God's throne, praising him, thanking him, and bringing our requests to him. He is the one we can go to for acceptance, love, strength, and help.

Week 47

💡 My Thoughts

Do I regularly bring my needs to God? _____

_____

_____

_____

_____

_____

_____

💗 My Prayer

"Holy and gracious Father, I praise you for giving me such a wonderful advocate and High Priest—your Son, Jesus. I praise you because you hear my prayers and want me to bring my requests to you. Thank you for loving me and forgiving me. Thank you for showing me mercy and grace. I ask you for your strength and wisdom to meet the needs I face today. Help me to honor you in my home. In Jesus's name I pray, amen."

This week I'm praying for:_____

_____

_____

_____

_____

_____

A Gracious Invitation

My Choices

- This week I will choose to start each day praising the Lord and taking my needs to him.

- This week I will choose to take my cares, worries, and needs to God throughout the day.

- This week I will choose to rejoice and rest in God's mercy and grace, which are always there to help me in times of need.

- This week I will choose to: _____

_____

_____

_____

_____

For Further Reading: Hebrews 3–5

> Beyond our utmost wants
> His love and power can bless;
> To praying souls he always grants
> More than they can express.
>
> JOHN NEWTON

Opportunities to Trust God

 Key Scripture: James 1:2–5

*Dear brothers and sisters, whenever trouble comes
your way, let it be an opportunity for joy. For when
your faith is tested, your endurance has a chance
to grow. So let it grow, for when your endurance
is fully developed, you will be strong in character
and ready for anything.*

*If you need wisdom—if you want to know
what God wants you to do—ask him, and he will
gladly tell you. He will not resent your asking.*

Learn how to suffer, for that is the most
important of all lessons.

François Fénelon

Opportunities to Trust God

 Mom's Reflection

Troubles are an opportunity for joy? Now, that's a positive perspective! According to James, we can count troubles as joy, because when our faith is tested, our endurance and perseverance have a chance to grow and make us stronger in character. Much like a muscle that is strengthened through resistance and pressure, we can grow in strength, wisdom, and maturity through our challenges.

That doesn't mean we should walk around all smiley faced when we go through troubles. But instead of grumbling, whining, and falling into despair, we need to see each trouble as an opportunity to trust God. It may not be easy, and we may not smile in the midst of it; but we can look at each situation knowing that God has a bigger plan, and he will help us grow through the experience. We can ask him for wisdom and guidance, and he will gladly answer us.

What trouble are you currently facing? Are you whining and grumbling about it, or are you looking at it as an opportunity to trust God and grow?

💡 My Thoughts

How can I grow through my current trials or challenges?

_____

_____

_____

_____

_____

_____

💜 My Prayer

"Wise and perfect Lord, I praise you, because I know you have a plan for my life, even through the struggles. I praise you, Father, because you are with me and you freely offer me wisdom and guidance. Thank you for strengthening me through adversity. Thank you for helping me to grow stronger. Help me to see every challenge as an opportunity to trust you. Lead me away from despair and into your warm embrace. In Jesus's name I pray, amen."

This week I'm praying for:_____

_____

_____

_____

_____

_____

Opportunities to Trust God

 My Choices

- This week I will choose to see my troubles as opportunities to trust God.

- This week I will choose to ask God for wisdom.

- This week I will choose to stop grumbling and start growing.

- This week I will choose to: _____

_____

_____

_____

_____

_____

For Further Reading: 1 Peter 2–5

Despise not the desert. There is where
God polishes his brightest gems.

R. A. Torrey

His Divine Power at Work

 Key Scripture: 2 Peter 1:3–8

As we know Jesus better, his divine power gives us everything we need for living a godly life. He has called us to receive his own glory and goodness! And by that same mighty power, he has given us all of his rich and wonderful promises. He has promised that you will escape the decadence all around you caused by evil desires and that you will share in his divine nature.

So make every effort to apply the benefits of these promises to your life. Then your faith will produce a life of moral excellence. A life of moral excellence leads to knowing God better. Knowing God leads to self-control. Self-control leads to patient endurance, and patient endurance leads to godliness. Godliness leads to love for other Christians, and finally you will grow to have genuine love for everyone. The more you grow like this, the more you will become productive and useful in your knowledge of our Lord Jesus Christ.

His Divine Power at Work

 ## Mom's Reflection

Did you ever turn on your blow dryer and nothing happened? When you followed the cord to its end, you realized that someone had unplugged it! Trying to use a blow dryer without electrical power is like trying to live a godly life without God's power. Peter assures us that as we get to know Jesus better, his divine power will give us everything we need for godly living. Isn't it wonderful to know that he will provide what it takes to live each day in a godly way?

We do have a part however. We can't just sit back and ignore our responsibility, saying, "Oh well, God's power will do it all." Peter is clear: God gives us his power, but we are responsible for applying it personally in our own lives. The end result? Lives that are positive and productive, useful and godly. I want that kind of life—and I want that kind of life for my kids. Don't you? Let's take the first step by drawing closer to Jesus and determining to know him better with each passing day.

My Thoughts

How can I personally draw closer to Jesus and know him better? _____

_____

_____

_____

_____

_____

💗 **My Prayer**

"Loving and powerful heavenly Father, I praise you, for your divine power gives me everything I need to live a godly life. Thank you for calling me to receive your own glory and goodness. Thank you for giving me your rich and wonderful promises. Let your light shine through me! Help me to live a productive and useful life according to your Word. Help me to know you better, and help me to teach my kids to know you better too. In Jesus's name I pray, amen."

This week I'm praying for:_____

_____

_____

_____

_____

_____

His Divine Power at Work

 My Choices

- This week I will choose to draw closer to God and seek to know him better.

- This week I will choose to recognize God's divine power at work in my life.

- This week I will choose to apply God's power personally, so that I might become a more godly woman and mom.

- This week I will choose to: _____

_____

_____

_____

_____

 For Further Reading: The Book of 2 Peter

> What God requires of us he himself works in us, or it is not done.
>
> MATTHEW HENRY

The Power of Love

 Key Scripture: 1 John 4:7–10

Dear friends, let us continue to love one another, for love comes from God. Anyone who loves is born of God and knows God. But anyone who does not love does not know God—for God is love.

God showed how much he loved us by sending his only Son into the world so that we might have eternal life through him. This is real love. It is not that we loved God, but that he loved us and sent his Son as a sacrifice to take away our sins.

The heart of him who truly loves is a paradise on earth; he has God in himself, for God is love.

LAMENNAIS

The Power of Love

 Mom's Reflection

What is real love? People throughout the ages have searched for soul-satisfying love in a myriad of ways. But as John tells us, there is only one place real love can be found: in a relationship with the God who first loved us. Real love is evidenced by the fact that God sent his Son, Jesus, as a sacrifice to take away our sins. As we receive his great love toward us, we are able to love him and love others.

Love comes from God. He *is* love. Love is not that warm, fuzzy feeling we get in our hearts when someone adores us and we adore them. It is much more secure and real. It's a gift we give based on actions, not on feelings. It's a choice we make. It's a command God gives.

Take a moment to reflect on God's great love for you. Enjoy it. Embrace it. Relish it! And as you do, choose to love others, because he—your heavenly Father—loved you first.

 **My Thoughts**

Am I enjoying God's love for me? Am I making a daily choice to love others? _____

_____

_____

_____

_____

_____

_____

My Prayer

"Loving heavenly Father, I praise you, because you are love. You defined love when you sent your Son, Jesus, as a sacrifice for my sin. Thank you for showering your love on me. Thank you that I can live confidently, knowing that I am completely loved by you. Please help me show real love—your love—to my children and to others. In Jesus's name I pray, amen."

This week I'm praying for:_____

_____

_____

_____

_____

_____

The Power of Love

 ## My Choices

- This week I will choose to thank God for his great love for me.

- This week I will choose to love the people around me; knowing that by doing so, I am pointing them to God.

- This week I will choose to teach my children about the source of real love.

- This week I will choose to: _____

_____

_____

_____

_____

_____

 For Further Reading: 1 Corinthians 13; The Book of 1 John

The greatest happiness of life is the conviction that we are loved, loved for ourselves, or rather loved in spite of ourselves.

VICTOR HUGO

Reaching Out with Mercy

 Key Scripture: Jude 20–23

But you, dear friends, must continue to build your lives on the foundation of your holy faith. And continue to pray as you are directed by the Holy Spirit. Live in such a way that God's love can bless you as you wait for the eternal life that our Lord Jesus Christ in his mercy is going to give you. Show mercy to those whose faith is wavering. Rescue others by snatching them from the flames of judgment. There are still others to whom you need to show mercy, but be careful that you aren't contaminated by their sins.

There is no exercise better for the heart than reaching down and lifting people up.

JOHN ANDREW HOLMES

Reaching Out with Mercy

 Mom's Reflection

When our family goes hiking, we usually encounter a few steep climbs along the way. Typically, my husband will go on ahead of us, gain a good foothold, then extend his hand and help the rest of us up. In our passage this week, Jude tells us to make sure we have a good foothold—a firm foundation in our faith. In other words, we need to know what we believe and live it out. We do that by studying God's Word, meditating on it, and obeying it. Then, as we gain a good foothold, we're able to turn and help others who are struggling in their faith.

Helping others takes more than a good foothold, however. It takes a merciful spirit. If you're like me, you've had times when you've looked at someone's sinful or foolish actions, crossed your arms, and said, "I can't believe they're doing that. I would never do that." Instead of crossing our arms, we need to open them up in a spirit of mercy and do what we can to keep that person from slipping and falling—without compromising or falling into sin ourselves, of course.

Let's continue to build our lives on the firm foundation of our holy faith. Then let's reach out mercifully, prayerfully, and carefully to help others gain a good foothold too.

Week 51

 My Thoughts

How can I strengthen my "faith foothold"? Who can I reach out to with God's mercy? _____

_____

_____

_____

_____

_____

My Prayer

"Merciful Father, I praise you for your Word! I praise you for giving me the wisdom and truth of the Bible as a sure foundation for my faith. Thank you for teaching me what to believe and how to live. Help me to live according to your Word. Help me to continue to build my life on a firm foundation of faith. Show me how to reach out to others in mercy. Keep me from stumbling myself, and use me to bring others to you. In Jesus's name I pray, amen."

This week I'm praying for:_____

_____

_____

_____

_____

_____

Reaching Out with Mercy

:slightly_smiling: **My Choices**

- This week I will choose to shore up my foundation of faith by reading God's Word.

- This week I will choose to show mercy to the people around me.

- This week I will choose to teach my children the importance of knowing what they believe.

- This week I will choose to: _____

_____

_____

_____

_____

 For Further Reading: Matthew 16–18

We cannot hold a torch to light
another's path without
brightening our own.

BEN SWEETLAND

A Longing for Heaven

 Key Scripture: Revelation 21:1–4

Then I saw a new heaven and a new earth, for the old heaven and the old earth had disappeared. And the sea was also gone. And I saw the holy city, the New Jerusalem, coming down from God out of heaven like a beautiful bride prepared for her husband.

I heard a loud shout from the throne, saying, "Look, the home of God is now among his people! He will live with them, and they will be his people. God himself will be with them. He will remove all of their sorrows, and there will be no more death or sorrow or crying or pain. For the old world and its evils are gone forever."

Heaven will mean the realization of all the things for which man was made and the satisfaction of all the out-reachings of his heart.

ERNEST F. KEVAN

A Longing for Heaven

 Mom's Reflection

There's a longing in my heart for heaven. Perhaps you have that longing too. The fact is, this world is not our home; we were created for a much better place. How wonderful to know that this is not all there is! God has a great plan that extends far beyond the here and now. He is preparing a place for us; and in this passage in Revelation, John gives us a glimpse of what it will be like. It's a place where God himself dwells among us. It's a place where there is no more sorrow, no crying, no pain, no death. It's a place where we will experience true, eternal joy—life more wonderful than we can imagine.

This is great news for us today, as moms, as wives, as Christian women. No matter what circumstances we are currently facing, no matter what pain we are presently suffering, we know there's hope up ahead. We were made for heaven! So while we journey here on earth for a time, let's faithfully continue to do the work God has given us, looking with joy toward our future home. Remember, our hope hinges not on what we have here; our hope is built on what is yet to come. For those of us who have put our faith in Christ, "happily ever after" will be a reality one day!

My Thoughts

What does knowing that I'm made for heaven mean to me in my daily life?_____

_____

_____

_____

_____

_____

♡ **My Prayer**

"King of kings and Lord of lords, I praise you, because you are worthy of praise. You are the High King of heaven, and you have a perfect plan. Thank you that I have a future and a hope with you. Thank you that what you have planned for me is far too wonderful to even imagine. I look forward to being with you one day in heaven. Until then, help me to be a positive mom who serves you with faithfulness, hope, and joy. In Jesus's name I pray, amen."

This week I'm praying for:_____

_____

_____

_____

_____

_____

A Longing for Heaven

 My Choices

- This week I will choose to praise the Lord for what he has planned for my future.

- This week I will choose to place my hope in heaven and not in the here and now.

- This week I will choose to teach my children what the Bible says about our heavenly home.

- This week I will choose to: _____

_____

_____

_____

_____

For Further Reading: Revelation 20–22

The human soul was made to enjoy
some object that is never fully given—
nay, cannot even be imagined as given—
in our present mode of subjective
and spatio-temporal experience.

C. S. Lewis

Never Underestimate the
Power
of a Positive
Woman!

This best-selling series by Karol Ladd offers you five ways to be a positive influence in the lives of those you love. One of the most amazing things about these books—the comment heard over and over—is that they share practical suggestions that are really doable!

Each of these books offers seven power-filled principles that will change the way you interact with others forever. In addition to these solid principles, each chapter includes four "Power Points":

- a *scripture* for you to read
- a *prayer* for power in your relationship
- a *verse* for you to memorize
- an *action step* to help you put your positive influence into action

Once you've read one, you'll want to read them all. You, too, can join the thousands of women who are becoming positive, powerful influences in the lives of their family and friends.

ISBN 1-58229-267-1

ISBN 1-58229-163-2

ISBN 1-58229-306-6

ISBN 1-58229-435-6

ISBN 1-58229-344-9

HOWARD
PUBLISHING CO.

Available where good books are sold.

The Power of a Positive Mom DVD

ISBN 1-58229-473-9

An Interactive Group Study
for Positive MOMS

Designed for a dynamic, interactive group study, these eight sessions will bring the power of a positive influence into the life of every woman who attends:

1. The Portrait of a Positive Mom
2. The Power of Encouragement
3. The Power of Prayer
4. The Power of a Good Attitude
5. The Power of Strong Relationships
6. The Power of Your Example
7. The Power of Strong Moral Standards
8. The Power of Love and Forgiveness

This easy-to-use DVD has been carefully designed so that anyone can facilitate a dynamic group session. No leadership training is needed.

The Power of a Positive Mom book complements the sessions on this DVD and is available wherever good books are sold.